FIGHT'S ON!

FIGHT'S ON!

Airborne With The Aggressors

TIM LAMING

Airlife
England

Jacket photographs
The jacket photographs are reproduced by permission of Mike Gapski (back top left), British Aerospace (back bottom left and right), remainder by Tim Laming

ACKNOWLEDGEMENTS

Although one might be forgiven for thinking that the number of aggressor and target facilities aircraft types is small, this is not the case. An astonishing variety of aircraft are used either regularly or occasionally as 'enemy simulators'. I have attempted to illustrate as wide a variety as possible, but the list of potentially appropriate aircraft is almost endless! My efforts to provide plenty of variety required the co-operation and assistance of many individuals, and I would like to thank some of them in particular: Scott Van Aken, Andy Hodgson, John Hale, Peter Foster, Ted Carlson, Glenn Ashley, Mike Gapski, Tom Walczyk and Paul Hoehn, together with the following: Royal Air Force Strike Command and Support Command Public Relations, Swiss Air Force Public Relations, Royal Navy Public Relations, Grumman and British Aerospace.

Tim Laming

Copyright © 1996 by Tim Laming

First published in the UK in 1996
by Airlife Publishing Ltd

British Library Cataloguing in Publication Data
A catalogue record for this book
is available from the British Library

ISBN 1 85310 410 8

All rights reserved. No part of this book may be reproduced or transmitted in any form or by any means, electronic or mechanical including photocopying, recording or by any information storage and retrieval system, without permission from the Publisher in writing.

Printed in Hong Kong

Airlife Publishing Ltd
101 Longden Road, Shrewsbury SY3 9EB, England

INTRODUCTION

Ask almost anyone to describe the role of a military aircraft, and the response will almost certainly be 'bomber' or 'fighter'. However, it's easy to identify many other tasks which the ubiquitous 'warplane' is designed to undertake, such as transport, reconnaissance, communications, training and so on. One particular role which receives relatively little public attention is that of the 'adversary' aircraft, the 'friendly enemy'. Realistically, the most effective training for a fighter pilot or an air defence radar, missile or gun operator would be to go to war against an aggressive enemy. Thankfully, the opportunities for such brutal 'on-the-job' training are fairly rare, and military planners have evolved a variety of peacetime training methods to give their personnel the most effective and realistic training opportunities possible.

Emphasis is placed upon simulation, attempting to reproduce the conditions of a 'real' wartime scenario, and it is this need for realism which has led to the widespread use of many military aircraft as pseudo-enemies, masquerading as marauding bombers or fighters during training missions and larger-scale exercises. Aircraft have always been used for this purpose to a greater or lesser degree, but it was during the early 1970s that the aggressor aircraft first became a familiar part of military aviation terminology. American experience in south-east Asia led to many changes in USAF and USN training and tactics, and after long years of peacetime training, America's fighter pilots were suddenly involved in a very real and brutal air war, in which many basic rules of aerial combat were quickly relearned.

It was widely accepted that a pilot's combat 'survivability' bore a direct relation to the number of combat missions he had flown. It was clear that real-time experience led to a greater effectiveness and a much better chance of living to fight another day, and so the adversary aircraft (with suitably experienced and well-trained instructors) quickly became a popular means of simulating aerial combat conditions. The United States Navy produced the now famous 'Ault Report', the 'Air-to-Air System Capability Review of 1968', which examined the reasons for the Navy's poor results in dogfights over Vietnam. Although the Navy (and the USAF) had a very capable fighter in the shape of the F-4 Phantom, an unrealistic emphasis had been placed on long-range radar interception techniques, which wrongly assumed that close-in 'dogfighting' was a thing of the past; Vietnam proved that this wasn't the case, and training concepts would have to be radically revised.

The 'Ault Report' (directed by Captain Frank W. Ault, former commander of the USS *Coral Sea*) led to the creation of 'The US Navy Postgraduate Course in Fighter Weapons, Tactics and Doctrine', an air-to-air combat training programme tailored to the needs of the Navy's Phantom crews. This rather unlikely title was eventually shortened to a more familiar name: 'Top Gun', which became the US Navy Fighter Weapons School. There was no doubt that the new approach to training worked, as the pre-Top Gun air-to-air 'kill' ratio over Vietnam was approximately 2:1. After the introduction of Top Gun it soared to 13:1.

The USAF's kill ratios remained disappointing however, and the Navy's Top Gun programme encouraged the Air Force to revise its own training methods, resulting in the USAF Fighter Weapons School and the world-famous 'Red Flag' exercises which concentrate not only on air-to-air combat, but the wider aspects of modern aerial warfare such as air-to-ground weapons delivery. Like the Navy, the USAF launched an investigation into their air-to-air results in Vietnam, and the 'Red Baron' report reached essentially the same conclusions as the Navy. In 1972 a six-aircraft flight (equipped with Northrop T-38 Talons) was formed at Nellis AFB, attached to the USAF Fighter Weapons School. On 10 October that year, the flight was expanded into the 64th Fighter Weapons Squadron, eventually becoming the 64th Aggressor Squadron, tasked with the specialised role of adversary training.

Outside the United States, aggressor flying has also become an increasingly important part of day-to-day training, although specifically tasked adversary aircraft are much less common. Almost every fighter mission requires the simulation of an interception profile, and fellow squadron pilots (often instructors) will assume the role of 'enemy' for the duration of the exercise. Using the same aircraft type ensures that both aircraft are perfectly matched in terms of performance (thus putting the emphasis on flying skills) and of course there are no additional costs which would be required to operate specialised aggressor aircraft. There are disadvantages however, not least the reduction in 'realism'. It's impossible to reproduce the handling qualities of a MiG-29 in a Tornado, for example.

Through the 1980s, many European nations were able to take advantage of the USAF's adversary training expertise, with a squadron of F-5Es assigned to the aggressor role being based in the UK (the F-5s were later replaced by F-16s). Although this unit (the 527th TFTAS) was primarily assigned to the support of USAFE units, many RAF and other NATO fighter squadrons were able to train with the Americans, their F-5Es closely resembling the size and performance characteristics of the MiG-21. Sadly, the end of the Cold War led to a huge reduction in USAF overseas presence, and the aggressor returned to the States, leaving the rest of NATO to rely completely on 'non-dissimilar' aerial combat training once more. A risky strategy perhaps, but one which was dictated by budget constraints rather than operational requirements. Today, there are no specifically tasked aggressor aircraft in Europe, and NATO's fighter squadrons use their own resources to

Over recent years, VF-126's Skyhawks appear to have adopted a policy of applying various national flags to the tail surfaces of their Skyhawks. The flags evidently represent potential adversary forces, and not surprisingly, the Iraqi flag has appeared on quite a few aircraft as illustrated by this A-4F on final approach to Miramar's runway in February 1992. *(Tim Laming)*

create realistic air combat scenarios. Pilots from each European country regularly train with each other, and these opportunities for joint training give fighter pilots some valuable time to fly and fight against a less predictable opponent.

The traditional adversary aircraft aside, there are also many other forms of aggressor flying which form an important part of modern military operations. The most technologically advanced is the electronic aggressor, the ECM (Electronic Countermeasures) platform which is designed to confuse enemy radio communications and radar transmissions. These 'electric jets' are designed essentially for combat operations, but during peacetime training the same aircraft are able to assume the role of an enemy radar/radio jammer, adding a significant amount of realism to almost any air exercise. As might be expected, the USAF and USN are major operators of ECM aircraft, but the type is also becoming increasingly common throughout NATO. The Royal Air Force, for example, has operated Canberras (strictly in the training role) as ECM aggressors for many years, and in 1995 this task was transferred to a civilian operator.

Finally, there is the less advanced but equally vital 'target aircraft', in the shape of unmanned drones and piloted target tugs. This type of aircraft has formed an important part of military training activity for many years, reaching back as far as World War Two. The ubiquitous target tug, as the name implies, is employed as a carrier aircraft for a variety of airborne targets which can be presented to land- or sea-based gunners, or airborne fighter pilots. These targets are often unsophisticated pieces of equipment, usually little more than a large banner or a wooden dart which can be trailed at a safe distance from the target tug, for fighter pilots to hone their cannon-firing skills. Alternatively, some relatively high-tech targets can be employed, and until recently the RAF operated the Rushton target which could simulate a high-speed, sea-skimming missile. Unfortunately, like so many other assets, the Rushton (and the carrier aircraft) has fallen victim to cost-cutting.

Many target tugs can also be used as passive targets, enabling gun and radar operators to track the aircraft without actually firing any weapons. In this role the target aircraft becomes a classic 'aggressor', assuming the role of an enemy attack aircraft, often streaking in towards ground defences at low level. The Royal Navy is a notable user of this type of system, having used Hunters for many years as low-level attack aircraft, representing enemy aircraft or missiles during naval exercises. Using the term 'target' more literally, some aircraft are specifically designed to be devoured by all kinds of weaponry as part of trials and development programmes, and during a limited number of 'live' exercises. Naturally, such aircraft are flown unmanned and these target drones (usually retired fighter types converted to the target role) are flown by a ground-based pilot via a radio communications link. The USAF operates a relatively large fleet of QF-106 fighters for this task, which are gradually consumed by missiles fired by F-15 and F-16 fighter pilots. Likewise, the Navy maintains a fleet of QF-4s for similar tasks, although the Navy's drones are more regularly assigned to missile trials rather than flying training exercises. In the UK, the Defence Research Agency operates a small fleet of Jindivik unmanned target drones which are used for missile trials and live firing during RAF Missile Practice Camps (MPCs).

Modern military aviation relies upon ultra-realistic training, and while technology enables ground-based simulation to handle some of these training requirements, there is still no alternative to the 'real thing'. Even the latest advances in 'virtual reality' are no substitute for strapping on a helmet, climbing into your jet and getting airborne. Consequently, the world of adversary flying, electronic aggressor support and target-towing remains vital to the effectiveness of every modern air arm, and the 'friendly enemy' looks set to remain flying in our skies.

F&W C-3605 SCHLEPP

One of the most unusual aircraft to enter military service, the C-3605 Schlepp was a specialised target tug operated exclusively by the Swiss Air Force. The aircraft was originally designed as the C-3603 fighter-bomber, employing a variety of unused Messerschmitt Bf109 spares. Powered by a Hispano-Suiza piston engine developing 1,200 hp, some 144 aircraft were manufactured between 1941 and 1944. The aircraft wasn't particularly successful as a fighter-bomber, and was relegated to second-line duties such as reconnaissance and, in particular, target-towing.

During 1967 the Swiss Air Force established that the C-3603 had potential for a further ten years of service life, and the remaining fleet was returned to the Federal Aircraft Factory (later F&W) for refurbishment. As part of this programme the aircraft were refitted with an Avco Lycoming T5307 turboprop engine (1,100 shp). In order to accommodate the lighter engine, the forward fuselage was lengthened, resulting in an unusually long nose section. The first refurbished airframe flew on 19 August 1968. A third (central) tail fin was also added to improve yaw stability, and ML Aviation supplied hydraulic winches with 6,500 feet of cable to equip the aircraft as a target tug. The cable runs from the rear cockpit through to the lower rear fuselage, and the resulting fit enabled the aircraft to tow illuminated targets at night.

The Swiss Air Force planned to convert twenty aircraft to 3605 standard, but eventually a total of twenty-three aircraft were produced between 1971 and 1973. Based at Sion, the aircraft remained active well beyond their expected ten years of service life, finally leaving the Swiss Air Force inventory when a small fleet of PC-9 target tugs was acquired. Most C-3605s were sold to civilian buyers and some are now airworthy as 'warbird' exhibits in the UK and the USA.

Switzerland operated a small number of F&W C-3605 Schlepps for target-towing duties until the 1980s, when the type was withdrawn from service. Although the turboprop powerplant might suggest that the aircraft is a fairly recent design, the Schlepp was built from surplus unused Messerschmitt Bf109 parts. Designed initially as a fighter-bomber, the type was quickly relegated to second-line target-towing duties, and served in this role for many years. Some of the retired airframes (such as this machine, pictured at Chino in 1990) found their way on to the civilian 'warbird' market. *(Tim Laming)*

FAIRCHILD A-10 THUNDERBOLT

Possibly the ugliest combat aircraft ever to see service with the United States Air Force, the ungainly A-10 Thunderbolt II is better known as the 'Warthog' for obvious reasons. However, its aesthetic qualities should not be confused with operational capability, as the A-10 has proved itself an outstanding combat aircraft. The A-10 was designed for the specific task of 'tank-busting', the Close Air Support mission, influenced by East–West relationships rather than the Vietnam War. In recognition of a formidable armoured threat from the (now-defunct) Warsaw Pact and North Korea (still a very real threat), the USAF issued a requirement in 1967 for a new CAS aircraft.

Authorisation was given for the production of two competitive designs, the Fairchild A-10A and the Northrop A-9A. The latter design was proved to be effective, but the USAF opted to order the even more impressive A-10 on 18 January 1973. The first A-10A made its maiden flight on 10 May 1972, the first production aircraft flying in February 1975. The first operational A-10 unit was created in April 1976. The A-10A became a distinctly European aircraft, with more than 100 aircraft assigned to the 81st Tactical Fighter Wing at RAF Bentwaters and RAF Woodbridge in the United Kingdom. The Wing was divided into six squadrons, all of which made regular detachments to forward operating locations (FOLs) in Germany. During 1988 two of these squadrons transferred to RAF Alconbury before participating in Operation 'Desert Storm'. However, the entire fleet of UK-based A-10s returned to the United States by 1983, following the end of the Cold War.

Currently, the A-10 is assigned to a variety of USAF units, not least the growing number of 'Composite Wings' which form part of the Air Combat Command inventory. The A-10 remains active in Germany, albeit in small numbers; however, the majority of A-10s saw service with the Air National Guard and Air Force Reserve. More recently the A-10 has begun to be replaced by ground attack-configured F-16s, although experience in the Gulf War appears to have discouraged the USAF from withdrawing the A-10 from service completely. The Warthog performed admirably during Operation 'Desert Storm', some 144 aircraft being deployed to the Gulf, assigned to Scud-hunting, anti-radar attacks, even air-to-air combat (shooting down two helicopters). Over 8,000 combat missions were flown with a mission-capable rate of 95.7 per cent. Despite such outstanding performance, the A-10 has never been a 'politically correct' aircraft, and has continually suffered from changes in defence strategy. Most importantly, the A-10 is often regarded as simply being 'too slow', despite the fact that the aircraft is heavily armoured and incredibly manoeuvrable. Desert Storm demonstrated that the fastest aircraft isn't necessarily the most effective.

BOEING B-52 STRATOFORTRESS

The mighty B-52 first flew on 15 April 1952, entering service with the United States Air Force Strategic Air Command in 1955 as an ultra-long-range nuclear bomber and eventually earning a place in aviation history as the longest-serving USAF warplane of all time. The Stratofortress was first used operationally during the Vietnam War, flying numerous conventional bombing missions during the 1965–1973 period. The early B-52A, B, C, D, E, and F models (easily identified by their distinctive tall tail fins) were gradually retired from USAF service during the 1970s, and by the beginning of the 1980s only the B-52G and B-52H remained in the USAF inventory.

Boeing manufactured a total of 193 B-52Gs at their Wichita, Kansas factory. With a shortened tail fin, increased fuel capacity (totalling 45,576 US gal), external fuel tanks and no less than eight Pratt & Whitney J57 turbojets, the huge 'Buff' was designed to carry the Douglas GAM-87A Skybolt air-launched ballistic missile, developed jointly by the USA and UK before the project was prematurely terminated. The G model could also carry North American GAM-77 (AGM-28) Hound Dog inertial-guidance stand-off missiles, and later in its career the aircraft was further modified to carry up to twenty AGM-69A SRAMs (Short Range Attack Missile) or ALCMs (Air Launched Cruise Missile), whilst still retaining a conventional bombing capability.

Earlier B-52 models featured a manned tail gunner position, but in the B-52G this system was replaced by a

LEFT:
The unmistakable shape of the Warthog, the Fairchild A-10A Thunderbolt II, if you prefer its proper name. Pictured out over the Arizona desert, with her refuelling receptacle open, *77-189* is from the 355th Fighter Wing based at Davis-Monthan AFB. The Warthog was a familiar sight and sound in the UK until the early nineties, when the A-10 was withdrawn from RAF Alconbury, Woodbridge and Bentwaters. Throughout the 1980s, Warthogs regularly participated in RAF exercises such as 'Elder Forest' and 'Mallet Blow', acting as hostile ground attack forces, and often giving Rapier SAM operators a very hard target to track. If you ever saw twelve Hogs attack an RAF base, you'll know what I mean! *(Curtiss Knowles)*

ABOVE:
The mighty Boeing B-52 couldn't be described as an 'aggressor' in the conventional sense of the word, but the Buff has traditionally assumed the role of a hostile bomber in countless exercises, including various 'Red Flag' events held over the Nellis AFB range in Nevada. This 1988 illustration shows a B-52G climbing away from Castle AFB in California, trailing the familiar plume of sooty smoke. Sadly, the B-52G has now been withdrawn from the USAF inventory. *(Mike Gapski)*

remotely controlled AN-ASG-15 fire control system, connected to four 12.7mm machine-guns. During Operation 'Desert Storm' the B-52G was employed on conventional bombing missions, delivering a total of 25,700 tons of munitions on targets in occupied Kuwait and in Iraq. The aircraft were operated directly from 'forward' bases at Jeddah (Saudi Arabia), Diego Garcia, Moron (Spain), and RAF Fairford, flying a total of 1,624 missions during the Gulf War.

Some 102 B-52H models were constructed for the USAF, the first example of the ultimate B-52 variant entering service in September 1960. The most obvious change incorporated into this variant was the change of powerplant to eight Pratt & Whitney TF-33-P-1 turbofans which improved the aircraft's performance, although the all-up weight of the airframe was substantially greater. The remaining B-52Gs were withdrawn from USAF service during 1994, leaving a USAF fleet of approximately ninety B-52Hs in service, assigned to both conventional bombing and AGM-86 ALCM missions, as part of the USAF's Air Combat Command.

MARTIN B-57 CANBERRA

The outstanding English Electric Canberra design greatly impressed USAF officials, and led to an order for a licence-built variant of the aircraft for light bomber duties with Tactical Air Command. A single aircraft was ferried to Martin's plant in Baltimore during 1951, where the manufacturer 'Americanised' the airframe, introducing US-built Armstrong-Siddeley Sapphire engines, Bendix combustion starters, and other construction features. The most radical change was made to the bomb-bay doors, which were replaced by a single rotating door which improved drag and gave bomb loads a cleaner separation.

The first Martin B-57A twin-seat bomber and reconnaissance aircraft made its first flight on 20 July 1953, but after the production of a small number of 'Alpha' models attention switched to the B-57B which featured a completely redesigned nose section with tandem seating arrangements under a one-piece hinged canopy. Rear fuselage door-type airbrakes were introduced and provision was made for wing-mounted guns (four 20mm or eight 12.7mm). Underwing hardpoints also gave the aircraft better ordnance-carrying capability.

The only export customer for the American-built Canberra was Pakistan, where former USAF machines continued to serve until the late 1980s on sea surveillance missions. Fitted with specialised maritime sensor equipment and surveillance radar, these aircraft were amongst the last active B-57s anywhere in the world. USAF B-57 operations ended in the 1980s when the last EB-57Bs were withdrawn from service with the Air National Guard. These aircraft had been assigned to the electronic countermeasures training role. The only remaining airworthy B-57s are assigned to the National Aeronautics & Space Administration (NASA), as two long-span RB-57 aircraft are still believed to be operational with the Agency, on ultra-high altitude reconnaissance duties.

BRITISH AEROSPACE BUCCANEER

Designed in the 1950s to meet a 1952 Admiralty requirement for a long-range carrier-based attack aircraft, the Buccaneer was specifically designed for high-speed ultra-low-level strike missions, operating at wavetop height below the sights of enemy radar systems. The B.103/NA.39 prototype first flew on 30 April 1958 from Blackburn's test airfield at Holme-on-Spalding Moor, having been manufactured at their Brough factory. The Buccaneer airframe was largely machined from solid castings, giving the aircraft immense strength, necessary for sustained low-level operations. The aircraft also took advantage of boundary layer control (BLC) technology, bleeding air over the wing and tailplane leading edges, and ahead of the flaps and ailerons, enabling the aircraft to operate at comparatively modest approach speeds, despite a fairly small wing planform.

The initial production variant was the Buccaneer S1 which, although a successful design, was underpowered (a pair of de Havilland Gyron turbojets). Take-off with a full fuel load was impractical which seriously restricted the aircraft's operational capabilities. The later S2 variant took advantage of more recent advances in engine design, and a pair of Rolls-Royce Spey turbofans gave the Buccaneer a combined thrust of 22,200lb. The first S2 made its maiden flight in May 1963, entering squadron service in April 1965. During January 1963 a batch of sixteen aircraft was ordered for the South African Air Force (designated Buccaneer S50). Delivered to the SAAF in batches of eight, the second group was transported by sea after one aircraft was lost during the first (air) delivery. An option for a further twenty aircraft was cancelled by the British Government following the

LEFT:
The EB-57E was a less sophisticated predecessor of the EF-111, dedicated to electronic warfare duties. This particular example served with the Vermont Air National Guard at Burlington international airport from 1974 until 1981, when the unit returned to fighter operations with F-4Ds (and now F-16s). Having earned an honourable retirement, she now forms part of an impressive museum collection (open to the public) at March AFB in California.
(Tim Laming)

ABOVE:
The Blackburn Buccaneer, in her element, low over the sea, skirting the coastline of the Orkneys in 1987. Designed as a low-level maritime attack aircraft, the Buccaneer was widely regarded as an outstanding aircraft. During many maritime exercises, Nos. 12 and 208 Squadrons mounted attack missions against a variety of NATO ships, providing radar operators with a very convincing representation of an enemy attack.
(Tim Laming)

imposition of an arms embargo, and the sixteen aircraft enjoyed a long and successful service until the late 1980s when the remaining Buccaneers were withdrawn from use.

The Royal Air Force showed little initial interest in the distinctly naval Buccaneer design, having expected to take delivery of the ultra-sophisticated TSR-2. Following the cancellation of that aircraft (and subsequently the F-111K), the RAF reluctantly opted to purchase the Buccaneer as a stop-gap aircraft until a more appropriate strike aircraft could be brought into service. However, the Buccaneer was ideally suited to RAF operations, and could out-perform the F-111K. Some twenty-six aircraft were ordered in addition to sixty-two aircraft which would be transferred from the Fleet Air Arm (and a further nineteen airframes were later ordered). Equipping Nos. 12, 15, 16, 208 and (briefly) 216 Squadrons, the Buccaneer enjoyed a long and hugely successful career with the RAF, both as an overland strike/attack aircraft and as a maritime-strike platform. The aircraft was finally (and reluctantly) withdrawn from RAF service in 1993, following the delivery of the first maritime-configured Tornado GR1Bs.

ABOVE:
Gear down, a Buccaneer crosses the Scottish coastline on final approach to home base at Lossiemouth. Tornado GR1Bs were assigned to the maritime attack role in 1994, when the last Buccaneers (with No. 208 Squadron) were retired. Many pilots insist that a suitably refurbished Buccaneer would perform the maritime attack role more effectively than the Tornado, but the faithful 'Brick' was a fairly 'old tech' machine, despite the fact that the last aircraft was delivered to the RAF as recently as 1977. At least one aircraft will hopefully remain airworthy as a warbird. *(Tim Laming)*

RIGHT:
The T-2C Buckeye is part of the aggressor community at Miramar, although the docile twin-engined trainer certainly isn't used for dissimilar air combat missions! VFC-13 fly the Buckeye on spin demonstration flights, enabling the aggressor pilots to explore extreme edges of the flight envelope without the risks that are associated with more 'temperamental' aircraft such as the Hornet. *(Tim Laming)*

ROCKWELL T-2 BUCKEYE

The history of the Buckeye can be traced back to 1956, when the United States Navy first issued a requirement for a basic jet trainer which could take students from the elementary stages of flying training through to more advanced activities such as carrier qualification and weapons delivery techniques. A number of companies submitted designs to meet this requirement, but North American Aviation was successful with its NA-249 design which drew upon earlier experience with the FJ-1 Fury and T-28 Trojan. The first YT2J-1 pre-production aircraft (no prototypes as such were built) flew for the first time on 31 January 1958.

Re-designated as the T-2A from 1962, the aircraft was powered by one Westinghouse J34-WE-48 turbojet, developing just 3,400 lb thrust, but the aircraft possessed a very impressive performance and some 201 aircraft were produced, the name 'Buckeye' being adopted in 1959 shortly before the aircraft entered service. The T-2A was the subject of further development, and two aircraft (designated YT2J-2) were converted to carry a pair of Pratt & Whitney J60-P-6 turbojets with a combined thrust of 6,000 lb. These aircraft eventually resulted in the T-2B which was adopted as a replacement for the T-2A, the first of ninety-seven production aircraft flying for the first time on 21 May 1965. The T-2B Buckeye entered service with VT-4 at Pensacola NAS in Florida during December 1965.

Further development of the T-2 resulted in the T-2C, powered by a pair of 2,950 lb thrust General Electric J85-GE-4 turbojets. Some 231 aircraft were constructed for the US Navy, the first example taking to the air on 10 December 1968. During 1982 a fleet of seventeen T-2Bs were removed from long-term storage and refurbished, eventually re-entering US Navy service to supplement the existing fleet of T-2Bs. A small number of aircraft were also converted to drone director standard, the 'Bravo' and 'Charlie' models being designated DT-2B and DT-2C respectively. Outside the United States, a total of twenty-four aircraft were purchased by Venezuela (designated T-2D), and these aircraft remain active with the Grupo de Entrenamiento, Aereo Escuela de Aviacion Militar, at Palo Negro, Maracay. Additionally, some forty aircraft were sold to Greece (designated T-2E), equipping Nos. 362 and 363 Miras, based at Kalamata, within the Greek Air Force Training Command. Deliveries of McDonnell Douglas T-45 Goshawks will gradually see the withdrawal of the T-2B/C from US Navy service.

BRITISH AEROSPACE CANBERRA

The world's first jet bomber made its maiden flight on Friday 13 May 1949 (the English Electric personnel obviously weren't superstitious) from the manufacturer's airfield at Warton in Lancashire. Designed as a high-level twin-seat bomber with a radar gunsight, the aircraft's mission was revised during the development stage and the Canberra entered service with a visual bombing system, requiring a clear glazed nose section, and a three-man crew. The aircraft relied on a relatively conventional design with two Rolls-Royce Avon engines situated outboard of the main undercarriage, semi-buried in the wing structure. The large-area wing was lightly loaded, giving the Canberra outstanding manoeuvrability which outclassed many fighter aircraft of the 1950s. Unfortunately the engine positioning also gave the Canberra its only major vice: a dangerous tendency to yaw in the event of an engine failure at low speed.

The early Canberra B2 bombers were later joined by more powerful B6 variants, followed by the B(I)8 interdictor, which featured a revised nose layout with the navigator inside the forward nose and the pilot positioned in a fighter-style canopy offset to port. The Canberra bomber fleet served the RAF with great distinction, being withdrawn in the 1970s as Phantoms, Harriers and Jaguars began to enter service.

The Canberra proved to be a versatile machine, developed into a wide variety of specialised variants and export versions beginning with the PR3, a photographic reconnaissance platform developed from the B2. The later PR7 was a similar development of the B6. Other Canberra variants included the TT18 target tug, T19 and T22 radar trainers, T4 twin-seat conversion trainer, and the extensively redesigned Canberra PR9 high-altitude reconnaissance aircraft. The PR9 features a B(I)8-style offset pilot's canopy (with the navigator housed in the

The DRA at Llanbedr operates this eye-catching Canberra, resplendent in a high-visibility MoD(PE) 'raspberry ripple' colour scheme, complete with black/yellow-striped 'target tug' undersides. *WH734* is a Canberra B2(MoD), used in support of various missile trials undertaken at nearby Aberporth. *(Tim Laming)*

ABOVE:
The eye-catching black and yellow stripes were traditionally applied to British target tug aircraft as part of a policy which began more than fifty years ago. However, the Canberra's Hawk replacements have not received these markings, despite the fact that they do occasionally carry targets and regularly act as passive 'silent' targets. The reason why this rather obvious flight safety measure has not been adopted remains unclear. *(British Aerospace)*

LEFT:
The well-weathered upper surfaces of the Canberra are visible in this picture, together with No. 100 Squadron's distinctive markings on her tail. The Canberra's fin was manufactured from wood, and is often slightly twisted to port or starboard, in order to compensate for the aircraft's slight longitudinal imbalance. Unlike modern warplanes, the Canberras were manufactured 'by hand', long before computerised technology ensured that every aeroplane is precisely the same as the next one! *(British Aerospace)*

nose section) and redesigned wing with extended span and inboard chord. The Avon engines are uprated 10,500 lb Avon 206 turbojets. Although the Canberra has virtually disappeared from Royal Air Force service, the PR9 remains active in small numbers with No. 39 (1PRU) Squadron at Marham, where the aircraft is retained for specialised photo-reconnaissance and mapping duties, together with a couple of Canberra T4 conversion trainers.

Perhaps the most unusual Canberra variant was the T17/A developed from the B2 for electronic countermeasures training. Fitted with a variety of radar and radio jammers and receivers (and chaff dispensers) the Canberra T17 remained in RAF service until late 1994, when ECM training activities were transferred to a civilian contractor.

RIGHT:
The world's oldest flying Canberra, *WD955*, pictured at Wyton during November 1991. A former B2, the aircraft was converted to T17 (and later T17A) standard, and continued to serve with No. 360 Squadron at Wyton until October 1994, when the squadron disbanded. The distinctive red tail with a yellow lightning flash is a one-off 'special', based on the squadron's more customary fuselage 'bar' markings. The hemp colour scheme reflects the squadron's reserve wartime role as a visual maritime reconnaissance unit. *(John Hale)*

LEFT:
High over the North Sea, a Canberra T17 from No. 360 Squadron, returning to Leuchars where the aircraft was deployed on an exercise with RAF Phantoms during 1989. The venerable Canberra is nearing the end of its service life with the RAF, although a small number of photo-reconnaissance aircraft are expected to soldier on for the foreseeable future. The Canberra ECM platform (and No. 360 Squadron) disappeared towards the end of 1994, when the ECM training task was passed on to a civilian contractor.
(Tim Laming)

BELOW:
Pictured en route to Leuchars during April 1989, a Canberra T17 is escorted by a Phantom FG1 from No. 111 Squadron. The Canberras provided the RAF with an effective ECM training facility, the aircraft acting as hostile 'aggressors' during small-scale interception sorties (such as this one), or during more elaborate air defence exercises. However, unlike the USAF, the RAF's ECM fleet was dedicated to training, and would not have been used in an operational context. By the end of 1994 the distinctive 'warty' Canberra was, like Treble One's Phantoms, consigned to memory. *(Tim Laming)*

LOCKHEED CONSTELLATION

One of the most significant airliner designs ever produced, the Lockheed Model 49 Constellation began life in 1939 when Howard Hughes (then in control of Transcontinental and Western Air) and Jack Frye (President of TWA) met with Lockheed's president Robert Gross and his engineers, Hall Hibbard and Clarence Johnson (the legendary 'Kelly' Johnson). TWA required a long-range and high-altitude transport capable of carrying 6,000 lb and a crew of six over a distance of 3,500 miles at 17,000 feet or higher. Lockheed proposed the Model 49, a design based on the earlier Model 44 Excalibur, with the wing design based on the successful P-38 fighter.

The Wright R-3350 Cyclone 18 piston engine was chosen as the powerplant, Lockheed opting for an excess of power in order to provide economy on long-range flights. However, the powerplant led to correspondingly large propellers, requiring an unusual curved fuselage structure and a stalky nose undercarriage for which the 'Connie' became famous. The Japanese attack on Pearl Harbor on 7 December 1942 temporarily halted development of the Constellation as a civil airliner, attention being switched to military transport applications for the design, known as the C-69. The prototype made its first flight on 9 January 1943 from Burbank, and the aircraft was delivered to the USAAF on 29 July 1943 for acceptance trials at Wright Field.

An initial order from TWA for nine aircraft was followed by a Pan American order for forty followed by another TWA order for thirty-one airframes. The USAAF ordered 180 before cancellations followed in 1945. The first civil Constellation (in TWA markings) was delivered to Las Vegas on 16 April 1944. With the advent of the Cyclone C-18 CB-1 engine delivering 2,700 hp, it became practical to develop the Constellation into a 'stretched' derivative, and the prototype L-1049 'Super Constellation' made its first flight on 13 October 1950, production aircraft entering service with Eastern Airlines in November 1951. A US Navy requirement for a long-range cargo/troop transport provided the basis for more military interest in the Constellation, and the later Wright turbo-compound Cyclone TC-18 DA-1 engine led to the development of the R7V-1, the first aircraft flying in November 1952. The Constellation proved to be an ideal transport aircraft for both the US Navy and USAF, and the aircraft was developed into a wide variety of variants for specialised tasks. The most important was perhaps the WV-2/EC-121 Warning Star airborne early warning platform which remained active with the USAF until 1978. Other aircraft were assigned to specialised tasks such as ECM training, weapons system tests, anti-submarine warfare, drone director and communications relay post.

ABOVE:
Moving back in time, the NKC-121 Constellation once served with VAQ-33 at Key West NAS in Florida, tasked with a variety of missions including electronic warfare 'aggressor' operations. Despite the addition of various lumps and bumps, the classic lines of the beautiful 'Connie' are still very much in evidence.
(Andy Hodgson collection)

RIGHT:
VAQ-34 operated the EA-7L Corsair on threat simulation missions from their home base at Point Mugu NAS in California, just a few miles north of Los Angeles. Following the withdrawal of the A-7 from other regular US Navy units, VAQ-34 also said goodbye to the 'SLUF', and re-equipped with F/A-18 Hornets.
(Mike Gapski)

VOUGHT A-7 CORSAIR

The A-7 Corsair was initially designed as a replacement for the US Navy and US Marine Corps A-4 Skyhawk attack aircraft which had served both services with distinction throughout the 1960s. Although the Skyhawk was a hugely successful design, both fast and manoeuvrable, it lacked range and load-carrying capability, and the A-7 was designed with these requirements as primary design considerations. Vought won the competition to manufacture the Skyhawk replacement in the form of a low-cost and relatively simple aircraft which could be put into production as quickly as possible. It was established that the new aircraft should be an adaptation of an existing design, and Vought's submission was based upon their successful F-8 Crusader supersonic fighter which was already in service with the USN and USMC. The primary change in design would be to adopt the un-reheated Pratt & Whitney TF30 turbofan which had been developed for the now defunct F-111B.

The A-7 retained the basic F-8 airframe configuration, but the Corsair was designed from the outset as a subsonic aircraft, becoming a shorter and fatter relative of the sleek Crusader predecessor. Speed became less of a priority when compared to the requirement for long range, and an impressive weapons carriage capability. Following the first flight of the prototype on 27 September 1965, some 199 A-7A variants were manufactured for the US Navy, the first examples entering service during October 1966. Although largely successful, the A-7A suffered from steam ingestion problems during catapult launches, reducing take-off weight. This problem was rectified with the arrival of the more powerful A-7B, and a total of 196 A-7Bs were built. Twenty-four of these aircraft were later converted to TA-7C tandem-seat dual-control trainer standard.

The improved A-7C (sixty-seven aircraft) was followed by the ultimate Navy A-7 version, the A-7E, of which more than 500 examples were manufactured. Powered by an Allison TF41-A-2 turbofan (a licence-built derivative of the Rolls-Royce Spey), the A-7E became the standard Navy Corsair throughout the 1980s until retirement shortly after the conclusion of Operation 'Desert Storm'. A small number of specialised aircraft remained active with the Navy, including the EA-7L, a twin-seat electronic warfare platform; however, the Corsair has now disappeared entirely from the USN/USMC inventory. Likewise, the A-7D (and twin-seat A-7K derivative) manufactured for the USAF has also been retired, after more than 400 examples completed more than twenty years of valuable service (the last A-7Ds having served with ANG units). Export examples continue to fly with both the Greek (A-7H) and Portuguese (A-7P) air forces.

MCDONNELL DOUGLAS F-15 EAGLE

The F-15 Eagle is perhaps the most capable and versatile fighter of the 1980s and 1990s, serving in large numbers with the United States Air Force, together with the air forces of Israel, Saudi Arabia and Japan. The design of this classic fighter dates back to 1965 when the USAF required a new long-range air superiority fighter. The FX programme led to the development of the F-15A which made its first flight on 27 July 1972, and during the following year an order was placed for the F-15A including a quantity of twin-seat, dual-control TF-15As (later redesignated F-15B). A total of 355 F-15As were constructed together with fifty-seven F-15Bs.

Operational service began with the first deliveries to Tactical Air Command's 1st Tactical Fighter Wing at Langley AFB, Virginia on 9 January 1976. The first Eagles to be deployed overseas joined USAFE at Bitburg AB in Germany, during April 1977. During 1974-5 McDonnell Douglas modified an F-15A airframe to capture a series of time-to-altitude climb records. The suitably stripped airframe named 'Streak Eagle' weighed 1,800 lb less than a standard F-15A and made eight successful record climbs, the most impressive being to 98,425 feet in 207.8 seconds from brake release on 1 February 1975.

From June 1979 the F-15A was replaced on the McDonnell Douglas production line by the F-15C (and twin-seat F-15D derivative). The 'Charlie' model is an improved version of the basic Eagle, with provision for conformal fuel tanks. Some 410 single-seat and sixty-one twin-seat aircraft were produced for the USAF. Earlier F-15A/B models were gradually assigned to Air National Guard and Air Force Reserve units as obsolete F-100, F-101 and F-106 aircraft reached retirement. Whilst still operational with TAC, some aircraft were modified to carry the ASAT anti-satellite weapon which was later cancelled before reaching the production stage, and these aircraft remain modified for the now defuct system.

The McDonnell Douglas F-15C Eagle, arguably the world's best fighter aircraft, and undeniably an outstanding interceptor and dogfighter. The USAF's Air Combat Command, USAFE and Air National Guard Eagle units participate in numerous exercises both in the United States and abroad, and the F-15 drivers are a pretty formidable force to be reckoned with, if you happen to be flying an opposing aggressor jet. *(Tim Laming)*

ABOVE:
Something of a nostalgic shot, with two F-15C Eagles returning to Bitburg in Germany after completing a one-versus-one air combat mission. After the departure of the UK-based USAF aggressor unit, the USAF (and other NATO forces) were forced to rely on their own units to provide crews and aircraft for air combat training. Although the forces of each nation do regularly train with each other, the true 'dissimilar air combat' package is no longer available. The USAF has now left Bitburg too, and the KC-135As are also long gone. *(Tim Laming)*

LEFT:
Returning to Nellis after completing a 'Red Flag' mission as part of the 'Red' force (the bad guys), an F-15A edges towards a refuelling tanker. No fancy airshow-type stuff here, just an honest snapshot which reveals some unusual 'pilot support' features, such as a drink carton, and what looks like a moose holding tightly on to the canopy! Who says fighter pilots don't have a sense of humour?! *(Curtiss Knowles)*

The F-15C/D is likely to be the subject of further improvement programmes and the USAF is considering a much-improved design (F-15XX) as a cheaper alternative to the F-22, should the latter programme be terminated. The older F-15A/B fleet will reach the end of their projected twenty-two-year lifespans shortly which will require the USAF to consider refurbishment options or retirement. The F-15 has also become a formidable strike/attack platform, developed from the twin-seat F-15B demonstrator, during the early 1980s. The first production F-15E Strike Eagle flew on 11 December 1986, entering operational service with the USAF during 1988. The Strike Eagle has largely replaced the F-111 in USAF ACC (Air Combat Command) service.

DOUGLAS EC-24A

Despite the fact that the Douglas DC-8 is an all-American airliner design, it wasn't until the 1980s that the type entered service with the United States armed forces. Just one example of the DC-8 was obtained by the United States Navy towards the end of the 1980s to supplement a pair of Boeing NKC-135As, operated by the Fleet Electronic Warfare Support Group (FEWSG) based at Waco in Texas. Designated EC-24A, the aircraft is assigned to the electronic warfare training role, providing the US Navy with representative 'hostile' radar and communications jamming during exercises at sea. Although precise details of the aircraft's equipment fit remain unknown, it is fitted with twin AN/ALT-40 jammers and an UN/USQ-113 communications intrusion, deception and jamming system.

In an interesting mix of manufacturer co-operation, the NKC-135s (and a pair of B-47E Stratojets previously assigned to the same role) were maintained by McDonnell Douglas (both aircraft types being Boeing designs) at a facility in Tulsa, Oklahoma, and it is likely that McDD's involvement in the Navy-contracted programme led to the acquisition of the DC-8 airframe. However, the three aircraft have now been re-contracted to the Chrysler Corporation, at their Waco facility in Texas.

The EC-24A is a DC-8-54F airframe powered by four Pratt & Whitney JT-3D-3 turbofans (each developing 18,000 lb thrust) extensively modified for the electronic countermeasures and electronic counter-countermeasures operations and features a bewildering array of 'lumps and bulges' scattered around the airframe, together with a proliferation of aerial blades. Identified equipment includes HF/VHF and UHF transceivers, dual HP-9826 mainframe computers, AN/ALR-75 Electronic Support Measures surveillance and detection equipment, and AN/ALE-43 chaff dispensers. Much of the EC-24A's systems remain classified, although it is known that the aircraft supports Fleet training exercises around the world, deploying to the Far East, and occasionally appearing in Europe, having visited the United Kingdom during 1994 for example.

The normal crew complement is seven (including mission specialists), although seating for an additional twenty personnel is available within the former airliner cabin.

ABOVE:
The unique EC-24A *163050* is a much-modified Douglas DC-8 airliner, refitted with a variety of packages for the electronic countermeasures and electronic counter-countermeasures duties. Operated on behalf of the Navy by the Chrysler Corporation based at Waco in Texas, the EC-24 (together with its two NKC-135 counterparts) provides training facilities for fleet units operating all around the world, acting as a sophisticated radar and communications-jamming 'aggressor'.
(Tim Laming)

OPPOSITE – TOP:
Not an aggressor, but a vital part of virtually every combat mission and air defence exercise. Aerial refuelling support has become a vital part of modern military air operations, and exercises such as 'Red Flag' are always supported by a variety of tanker forces. This KC-10 Extender was pictured during 1993, after having refuelled a flight of F-15 Eagles which had previously drained their tanks almost to empty during an air combat manoeuvring mission. *(Curtiss Knowles)*

MCDONNELL DOUGLAS KC-10 EXTENDER

Developed in response to a United States Air Force requirement for an advanced tanker/cargo aircraft (ATCA), the KC-10A was selected in December 1977, some sixteen aircraft being ordered, eventually increasing to a total of sixty. The KC-10A is a militarised tanker and cargo-carrying conversion of the McDonnell Douglas DC-10-30CF airliner with a truly strategic capability, carrying up to 169,409 lb of cargo over a range of 4,370 miles without in-flight refuelling (although the aircraft is equipped to receive fuel in flight). The KC-10 enables the USAF to support fighter deployments around the world, carrying appropriate support equipment and refuelling the fighters en route to their destination.

The lower section of the KC-10 (beneath the cargo floor) is fitted with bladder fuel cells which increase the total amount of on-board fuel to 54,455 US gal. The fuel is transferred to receivers from the boom operator's position at the extreme lower rear fuselage. Unlike the cramped couch positions in the KC-135, the Extender's 'office' is a very civilised arrangement with rearward-facing seats, from where the McDonnell Douglas AARB (Advanced Aerial Refuelling Boom) is controlled. A refuelling HDU (Hose Drum Unit) is located next to the boom, enabling the KC-10 to refuel probe-equipped USN and USMC aircraft and aircraft from other NATO forces. The Extender fleet is also gradually receiving underwing refuelling pods which will give the aircraft a three-point tanker capability similar to the Royal Air Force's VC10 fleet.

In the strategic transport role the Extender can carry up to twenty-five 463L pallets or alternatively a mixed load of pallets and passengers, the total useable cargo space being some 12,000 cubic feet. Normal crew for the KC-10A is four, comprising pilot, co-pilot, flight engineer and boom operator. The Extender's inertial navigation systems makes a navigator unnecessary. Unlike the KC-135 however, the KC-10 is not assigned to the support of operational strategic bomber missions, lacking shielding against electromagnetic pulses and thermal blast curtains.

Powered by three 52,500 lb thrust General Electric CF6-50C2 turbofans, the KC-10A has a maximum level speed of 610 mph and a ferry range of 11,500 miles. The KC-10A made its first flight on 12 July 1980, making the first aerial refuelling on 30 October of the same year (the recipient was a C-5 Galaxy). The first Extender to be delivered to the USAF arrived on 17 March 1981 and currently equips the 32nd ARS at Barksdale AFB, Louisiana, the 6th and 9th ARS at March AFB, California, and the 344th/911th ARS at Seymour-Johnson AFB, North Carolina. Aircraft are also assigned to Composite Wings and regularly accompany overseas deployments.

GENERAL DYNAMICS F-111

Although the F-111 is hardly at the forefront of modern warplane technology, it still forms a major part of the USAF's strike/attack capability, with a sizeable fleet of aircraft based at Cannon AFB in New Mexico as part of Air Combat Command. In some respects it is superior to its replacement aircraft, the F-15E Strike Eagle, and although there are continued rumours of possible withdrawal, the F-111 remains operational.

The F-111 was developed from the TFX (Tactical Fighter, Experimental) requirement issued in 1961, a project intended to produce a multi-role fighter for both the USAF and US Navy. The prototype YF-111A made its first flight on 21 December 1964 and was followed by seventeen pre-production development aircraft, leading to 141 F-111A aircraft which were delivered to the USAF, starting in June 1967. The naval F-111B was an unsuccessful project and US Navy interest in the aircraft ended after only nine aircraft had been built.

Only one export customer for the 'Aardvark' was secured, some twenty-four aircraft being manufactured for Australia, designated F-111C. The aircraft were essentially similar to the F-111A, but featured the longer-span wings of the F-111B together with strengthened landing gear and eight underwing weapons pylons (instead of four). The F-111E was an improved version of the 'alpha' model, with uprated engines and larger engine intakes intended for the later TF30-P-100 engine (fitted to the F-111F). The F-111D featured improved avionics, followed by the F-111E, a more powerful and very capable aircraft. The F-111F force was eventually concentrated at RAF Lakenheath, and performed a series of attacks on Libya during April 1986, before participating heavily in Operation 'Desert Storm' (the F-111F Wing was replaced by F-15Es during 1993).

The FB-111A entered service with SAC during 1969 as a strategic bomber equipped with AGM-69 SRAM missiles and a variety of free-fall nuclear bombs. A small proportion of the FB-111A fleet was later converted to F-111G standard, joining the Aardvark fleet at Cannon AFB. The F-111K was a designation applied to aircraft destined for the Royal Air Force following cancellation of the TSR-2 programme. The F-111 order was also cancelled at a later date. In addition to strike/attack-dedicated F-111s, the USAF continues to operate the EF-111 'Raven', a Grumman conversion of the F-111A designed for ECM operations. Used for strike package escort missions or stand-off jamming, the EF-111A is an ultra-capable communications and radar suppression platform.

The EF-111A Raven, better known as the 'Spark Vark', is a Grumman conversion of the basic General Dynamics F-111A airframe, providing the USAF with a dedicated electronic warfare communications and radar jamming platform. Although the type was operated within Europe (as part of the Upper Heyford Aardvark fleet), the Ravens were withdrawn to the United States, and the two squadrons of aircraft at Mountain Home AFB in Idaho are in the process of moving south to Cannon AFB in New Mexico, the remaining home of the F-111. *(Ted Carlson)*

LOCKHEED F-16 FIGHTING FALCON

The NFWS currently operates a mixed fleet of F/A-18 and F-14 aircraft in support of a busy schedule of aerial combat training missions. The Lockheed F-16N Fighting Falcon has replaced the F-5E/F fleet previously operated by the unit. This twilight image illustrates clearly the F-16's gold-tinted canopy, and the single AIM-9 Sidewinder missile training round attached to the port wingtip. *(Tim Laming)*

The most numerous USAF combat aircraft of the 1990s, the F-16 first flew as the YF-16 prototype on 8 December 1976. Designed as a lightweight ultra-manoeuvrable fighter, the aircraft was selected by the USAF after a fly-off competition with the Northrop YF-17 Cobra, which was later developed by McDonnell Douglas into the F/A-18 Hornet. Eight development aircraft were ordered by the USAF including a twin-seat F-16B which retains the same capabilities as the single-seater at the expense of slightly reduced fuel capacity. During June 1975 the F-16 was chosen by Belgium, the Netherlands, Denmark and Norway as a replacement for their fleets of ageing F-104 Starfighters, effectively making the Fighting Falcon the 'Eurofighter' of the 1980s and 1990s.

Delivery of operational F-16s began in January 1979 when the first aircraft were assigned to the 388th TFW at Hill AFB, Utah. The early F-16A model, powered by a Pratt & Whitney F100 turbofan, was later joined by the more advanced F-16C (and the twin-seat F-16D counterpart) powered by a General Electric F110 engine. The USAF now operates a mixed fleet of F-16A/Cs, divided into a variety of Block Number batches, each with differing powerplant and equipment changes. One of the most obvious airframe improvements is the extended horizontal stabilator which offers greater manoeuvrability. Likewise, the F-16C features an enlarged tail-fin lower leading edge, designed to house an airborne self-protection jammer system (which was later abandoned).

Initial production versions of the F-16A now mostly serve with ANG and AFRES units, designated as F-16A(ADF) Fighting Falcons. The 'ADF' refers to 'Air Defense Fighter', these aircraft being distinguishable by an avionics bulge at the base of the tail-fin. The later F-16C/D has also been given a night attack capability and the aircraft is assigned to a variety of air defence and ground attack missions. The F-16 also equips the USAF world famous 'Thunderbirds' Air Demonstration Squadron based at Nellis AFB, Nevada. Also located at Nellis AFB is the 57th FFW which operates a small fleet of F-16s assigned to aggressor flying duties in support of Red Flag exercises. Export sales of the F-16 have been hugely successful, and the aircraft continues in production. US Navy interest in the F-16 began when the aircraft first competed with the YF-17 design (which was later chosen by the Navy, as explained previously). The USN did eventually purchase twenty-six examples of the F-16 (designated F-16N), four of which are twin-seat TF-16N trainers. The first aircraft was delivered during April 1987 and are similar to the USAF F-16C, minus the internal cannon and underwing weapons stations. The aircraft are assigned to aggressor flying duties with the NFWS, VF-126 and VF-45.

RIGHT:
Topgun also operated a small number of twin-seat TF-16N Fighting Falcons, as illustrated by this early evening view. Note the F-16's tail-mounted airbrakes either side of the tail, in the extended position.
(Tim Laming)

BELOW:
Like many other adversary aircraft, *163269* isn't quite what she seems. Okay, it *is* an F-16, but the United States Marine Corps doesn't operate the Fighting Falcon. This particular aircraft, pictured in Canada during June 1990, belonged to Topgun, but carries 'Marines' titles in recognition of the USMC pilots who are always present at the NFWS. The colour scheme appears to represent the Swedish-style splinter pattern, although Sweden is naturally not regarded as a potential adversary, so the reasons for this bizarre paint job remain unclear. Maybe it just looked good?!
(Scott Van Aken)

ABOVE:
Over on the east coast, Oceana NAS in Virginia is the home of the Atlantic Fleet Tomcat squadrons, and as might be expected, the base was also home to an aggressor unit. VF-43, the 'Challengers', operating a mixed fleet of F-16N, TF-16N, F-5E and F-5F aircraft. One of the resident F-16Ns is pictured on the Oceana ramp, baking under the hot Virginian sunshine in front of the base control tower. *(Tim Laming)*

LEFT:
Resplendent in an eye-catching 'desert' colour scheme, an F-16C returns to Nellis after completing an ACM mission as part of a 'Red Flag' exercise. Although the US Navy appears to value dissimilar air combat training (if the number of aggressor-assigned aircraft is an indication), the USAF evidently favours inter-squadron air combat training, relying on regular squadron pilots to fly against one another. Whether this kind of training is less effective is open to question, but it is almost certainly less expensive.
(Mike Gapski)

ABOVE:
By July 1989, when this photograph was taken, the 527th AS had moved from Alconbury to RAF Bentwaters, and had re-equipped with the F-16C Fighting Falcon. Sadly, the 527th enjoyed only a short association with the F-16, as the USAF later disestablished the unit. By 1994 the USAF had left Bentwaters completely, and only the memories of Voodoos, Phantoms, A-10s and F-16s remain at this now disused airfield. *(Tim Laming)*

RIGHT:
Unusual rear view of a Royal Netherlands Air Force F-16A, as seen from the cockpit of another Fighting Falcon. Dutch F-16s are regular visitors to the United Kingdom, participating in exercises and squadron exchange programmes. The agile F-16 provides RAF Tornado pilots with a formidable 'friendly enemy' opponent, especially when compared to the RAF Tornado F3's relatively modest manoeuvring performance. *(RNLAF)*

IAI F-21 KFIR

Although France was a traditional supplier of arms to Israel, increasingly poor relations between the two countries prompted Israel to consider mating the American-manufactured General Electric J79 reheated turbojet to their fleet of Mirage III/5 airframes. The match was successful, and the first converted aircraft (named 'Kfir', or Lion Cub) was flown for the first time in June 1973. The airframe (an Israeli Nesher) was essentially a Mirage 5 with a shortened rear fuselage with increased diameter to house the larger American engine. The only other major modification was a large dorsal intake ahead of the vertical tail. Internally, the avionics system was completely changed, transforming the aircraft into a multi-mission fighter, capable of carrying Rafael Shafrir 2 AAMs whilst retaining a pair of DEFA 30mm cannon for close air combat.

Two IAF squadrons re-equipped with the Kfir C1 in 1976, seeing combat over Israel's northern borders during the following year. Meanwhile an improved version of the aircraft (Kfir C2) had entered production, externally distinguishable by a pair of canard foreplanes ahead of the wing leading edges, improving air combat manoeuvrability and take-off/landing performance. Approximately 200 aircraft were produced between 1976 and 1980, some of the original Kfir C1s being converted to C2 standard.

The Kfir C2 was exported to both Colombia and Ecuador in small numbers, but most unusually, the Kfir also entered service with both the United States Navy and Marine Corps. Following a decision to upgrade the capabilities of USN/USMC aggressor squadrons, a fleet of Kfirs was leased from Israel as an interim adversary aircraft, pending delivery of F-16Ns. These aircraft, designated F-21A, entered service in April 1985 for a period of approximately three years, operating with VF-43 at Oceana, and VMFT-401 at MCAS Yuma. Following the delivery of F-16Ns to the US Navy, surplus F-5E/Fs were transferred to the USMC, enabling the F-21 fleet to be returned to Israel.

VMFT-401 was the USMC operator of the Israel Aircraft Industries F-21 (Kfir C2) as illustrated by this September 1987 picture of a two-tone grey camouflaged example. Some machines were painted in brown 'desert' camouflage. *(Scott Van Aken)*

NORTHROP F-5E/F TIGER II

The F-5E is perhaps the most well-known aggressor aircraft of all time, having served with a variety of USAF, USMC and USN units around the world in the Dissimilar Air Combat Training (DACT) role. Although the Tiger is now disappearing from widespread service as an aggressor, the type remains active, most notably with the United States Marine Corps. The F-5E's history can be traced back as far as 1955, when Northrop initiated the development of the T-38 Talon twin-seat supersonic trainer and the F-5A Freedom Fighter, which first flew in May 1963.

This lightweight, low-cost, simple and reliable fighter was quickly adopted by a number of countries, not least because of the United States' ongoing Military Assistance Program, of which the F-5 became a part. Surprisingly, however, there was little interest in the type from either the USAF or Navy, and it wasn't until the later F-5E version was produced that Northrop's design finally began to secure obvious home-grown interest. The F-5E is essentially an 'improved F-5A' with more powerful engines, wider wingspan, an extending nosewheel (contributing to a better take-off performance), and better all-round capability. Flying for the first time in August 1972, the F-5E entered service with the USAF's 425th TFTS during April 1973.

Although the Tiger was initially adopted by the USAF as a lightweight tactical fighter, the type was quickly introduced into the aggressor training role, first with the 64th and 65th Aggressor Squadrons at Nellis AFB, and then with the 527th Aggressor Squadron and 26th

Northrop F-5E *159882* is pictured in front of a particularly famous hangar, the home of the United States Naval Fighter Weapons School at Miramar Naval Air Station, California. The famous Paramount movie starring Tom Cruise gave worldwide fame to the unit's alternative unofficial name, and 'Topgun' has almost become a household word. The NFWS is destined to leave Miramar, moving north to Fallon NAS in Nevada. *(Scott Van Aken)*

ABOVE:
The 'Desert Bogeys' acquired their F-5Es during 1987, when other Navy aggressor units exchanged their F-5s for F-16s. VFA-127 also received some F-5s from the USAF, when the 527th Aggressor Squadron also re-equipped with F-16s in 1988. The fast and agile F-5 enables the 'Bogeys' to represent the flight characteristics (and size) of aircraft such as the MiG-21. *(Tom Walczyk)*

LEFT:
You probably don't need reminding that the 'bad guys' in the movie *Top Gun* flew a variety of 'MiG fighters' which looked suspiciously like F-5Es? Well, you also probably know that the F-5Es were borrowed from the NFWS, and were covered with black latex paint especially for their film role. Although these aircraft were quickly restored to their more traditional colours after the filming ended, VFA-127 later painted up one of their F-5Es in the same all-black scheme, which turned more than a few heads at air shows all around the USA and Canada whenever she appeared. The fancy paint scheme didn't have any real combat training value, but it was a great public relations medium. *(Tim Laming)*

Aggressor Squadron at Alconbury (UK) and Clark AFB (Philippines) respectively. The US Navy first acquired the type during the mid-1970s, when five former Vietnamese examples were delivered to the USN Fighter Weapons School (Top Gun), and by the end of that decade, Miramar was host to a relatively large number of F-5E aggressors. More aircraft were acquired when the USAF withdrew the type and concentrated aggressor training at Nellis AFB (with a handful of F-16s).

The F-5E's high-speed capability, manoeuvrability and small size made the aircraft an ideal 'bogey', closely matching the visual characteristics of aircraft such as the MiG-21. Tigers served with VF-45 and VF-43 on the East Coast, together with VFA-127 at Fallon NAS (where the type remains active alongside F/A-18s, albeit in relatively small numbers). Having been replaced by F-16s at Miramar, the type is still active in the skies over California, as VMFT-401 at MCAS Yuma continues to fly the Tiger in the aggressor role, in support of various USMC combat units. The twin-seat F-5F (which retains the same performance as the single-seater) also remains active.

The F-5E Tiger remained active with VF-43 despite the arrival of the F-16N, and a small number of A-4F and TA-4J Skyhawks were also active with the unit until 1993. VF-43 was disestablished in 1994, handing the aggressor task to co-located VFC-12. One of the 'Challengers'' Tigers is pictured taxying back to the Oceana ramp in June 1992, after completing an ACM mission. *(Tim Laming)*

LEFT:
Up in the air over Fallon NAS, a gaggle of F-5Es from VFA-127 sweep over the airfield after completing an ACM mission. The F-5E is gradually disappearing from VFA-127's inventory as more modern F/A-18 Hornets arrive. Air Wings from both the east and west coast deploy to Fallon for work-up training prior to embarking upon cruises, and rely upon VFA-127 to provide them with dissimilar air combat training facilities. *(Tom Walczyk)*

BELOW:
The United States Marine Corps also maintains a fleet of aggressor aircraft. A small number of Skyhawks are assigned to Marine Aviation Logistics Squadrons for various support duties, including dissimilar air combat. However, the primary USMC aggressor unit is VMFT-401, the 'Snipers', based at Yuma in Arizona. The unit operates a large fleet of F-5E and F-5F Tigers, painted in a variety of eye-catching camouflage schemes, supporting various USMC fighter and attack units based at, or deployed to, Yuma. *(Gary Meinert)*

RIGHT:
The United States Air Force was, until fairly recently, a major advocate of dissimilar air combat training, with various aggressor units active both in continental USA and overseas. However, a mixture of cost-cutting measures and revised training policies has seen the USAF aggressor fleet reduced almost to zero. The only remaining aggressor fleet is now based at Nellis, where a small number of aircraft are assigned to the ongoing series of 'Red Flag' exercises. This March 1989 picture recalls the heyday of USAF aggressor operations, when the F-5E was active at Nellis AFB with the 57th FWW in relatively large numbers. *(Mike Gapski)*

BELOW:
Switzerland is also a major operator of the Northrop F-5E Tiger, two examples of which are seen high above the clouds, fitted with wingtip-mounted AIM-9 Sidewinder training rounds. For many air combat manoeuvring sorties, the F-5s carry dayglow orange-painted under-fuselage fuel tanks, flying ACM missions against other F-5s or against Mirage interceptors.
(Tim Laming)

FIAT G91

December 1953 saw the appearance of a NATO requirement for a light tactical support and fighter aircraft which generated proposals from a number of European aircraft manufacturers. Italy's FIAT was the eventual successful company, after trials were conducted at Bretigny in France during the autumn of 1957. Their prototype G91 was evaluated after making its first flight on 9 August 1956 and the trials in France proved that the aircraft was more than capable of meeting the NATO requirement, with a good capacity for external ordnance carriage and rough field operations.

The G91 entered service in February 1959 with 103 Squadriglia of the Aeronautica Militare Italiana, as a ground attack fighter, although the development of a photo-reconnaissance version of the 'Gina' was already underway, and this variant (designated G91R) flew during the same year. Although similar to the initial production version, the G91 featured a shortened nose section containing three 70mm Vinten cameras. The G91R/1 entered service with the AMI, the G91R/1A being an improved version with better navigation aids. The G91R/1B featured a strengthened airframe and equipment changes, whilst the G91R/3 (manufactured for West Germany) was fitted with two 30mm cannon, a Doppler radar and other navigational improvements. Finally, the G91R/4 featured further armament and minor equipment modifications.

The 'Gina' served with the Luftwaffe for many years, the final examples being operated by a civilian unit on target facilities duties. Italy retained examples of the G91R until the early 1990s when they were retired, although twin-seat G91Ts remain active in small numbers. Portugal also retained a G91R fleet until the early 1990s when the final examples were retired following deliveries of former Luftwaffe Alpha Jets. Greece and Turkey were allocated G91s under the US MAP scheme, but their aircraft were diverted to Portugal and Germany. Likewise, ten examples were evaluated by the USAF although the type never entered service.

The G91Y was a twin engine development of the basic G91 airframe, designed to meet an Italian requirement for a new lightweight ground attack fighter. Based on the lengthened G91T airframe, the two General Electric J85-GE-13A engines gave the G91Y a combined thrust of more than 8,000 lb which enabled the aircraft to carry more external weapon loads over longer distances. Deliveries of AMXs have enabled Italy to retire most of the G91Y fleet.

The diminutive Fiat G-91 tactical support aircraft served with the West German, Italian and Portuguese air forces for many years, and small numbers of 'Ginas' remain active in Italy. Germany's association with the delightful little Gina ended in 1992 when Condor Flugdienst (based at Husum) disposed of its target tugs, which were flown on behalf of the Luftwaffe until PC-9s were acquired as replacements.
(Fritz Becker)

BRITISH AEROSPACE HARRIER

First entering service with the Royal Air Force in 1969, the Harrier was the world's first fixed-wing vertical/short take-off and landing aircraft. The initial Harrier GR1 variant was upgraded to GR3 standard, incorporating a new nose section housing a Ferranti LRMTS (Laser Ranging and Marked Target Seeker), and RWR (Radar Warning Receiver) equipment in a revised tail configuration. The Harrier GR3 remained in RAF service until 1994, the last pair of aircraft remaining active until shortly after the type's twenty-fifth anniversary of entry into RAF service.

McDonnell Douglas purchased the rights to Harrier development and produced the AV-8B, a radical redesign for the basic Harrier airframe, using an uprated version of the original Pegasus powerplant, and with a fifty per cent increase in fuel capacity, a seventy per cent increase in ordnance capability, and a sixty per cent improvement in maintenance man hours. British Aerospace produced the AV-8B for the RAF under the designation Harrier GR5, the first developmental aircraft flying in April 1985, and the first production machine entering RAF service in July 1987.

ABOVE:
The RAF Harrier force plays an important part in many exercises, flying attack profiles against airfields, SAM units and radar sites around the UK. The Harrier GR7 is capable of carrying a pair of AIM-9 Sidewinder missiles, giving the aircraft an effective self-protection capability. The Harrier is, by its very nature, a very agile combat aircraft, and ACM engagements with other fighter types are often fairly equally matched. *(Tim Laming)*

RIGHT:
A very unusual picture of a very unusual formation. The Harrier is, of course, a very capable ground attack aircraft, but the new-generation Harrier GR7 also has an impressive air-to-air capability which, although primarily a defensive capacity, could really ruin a hostile fighter pilot's day! Harrier pilots occasionally practise their AAM firing skills over the Aberporth range in Wales, launching Sidewinders against Jindivik RPVs (Remotely Piloted Vehicles). This post-attack picture brings the 'fighters' and target together for the first time. *(British Aerospace)*

The Harrier GR7 is a night-attack development of the Harrier GR5 (and the interim GR5A version) featuring a FLIR (Forward-Looking Infra-Red) system which connects with the pilot's NVGs (Night Vision Goggles), giving the aircraft the ability to operate by day or night in virtually all weather conditions except thick fog. The GR5 fleet has been progressively upgraded to GR7 standard. Weapons options include 1,000 lb free-fall and retarded bombs, BL.755 cluster bombs, type 155 rocket pods (each containing 18 x 68 mm rockets) and Paveway laser-guided 1,000 lb bombs. The Harrier GR7 fleet will also eventually receive the twin Aden 25mm cannon (each with 100 rounds) which is currently under development.

The Harrier GR7 also has a reconnaissance capability, with a Vinten VICON 18 series 403 pod attached to the centreline hardpoint. The pod contains a Vinten 4000 infra-red linescan camera and a type 753 panoramic camera, and a VICON 57 pod can be carried for long-range oblique photography. Self-protection measures include AIM-9L Sidewinder AAMs and BOL-34 chaff/flare dispensers. The Harrier T4 dual control trainer is a tandem-seat trainer derivative of the Harrier GR3, and remains in service until a batch of new-build Harrier T10s are delivered to the RAF during the mid-1990s. The Harrier T10 is a dual-control version of the Harrier GR7 retaining the latter's combat capability.

BRITISH AEROSPACE HAWK

A total of 176 Hawks were ordered by the Royal Air Force as replacements for the fleet of Gnat and Hunter aircraft used for advanced flying and tactical weapons training. The first aircraft made its maiden flight on 21 August 1976 with deliveries to the RAF beginning in November of the same year. Although the Hawk is employed primarily as an advanced trainer within the RAF, it has a reserve wartime role as a visual point-defence fighter which would operate as part of a Mixed Fighter Force (MFF) concept, alongside radar-equipped (but less agile) Tornado F3s. Hawks currently equip No. 4 Flying Training School at RAF Valley, where graduates from Nos. 1 and 3 Flying Training Schools (flying Tucano basic trainers) progress on to advanced flying training activities and tactical weapons operations. The FTS is divided into three units, these being Nos. 19(R), 74(R) and 208(R) Squadrons. Hawks also form part of No. 6 Flying Training School, used for low-level and high-speed navigator training, while No. 100 Squadron flies the Hawk on target facilities missions, both units being based at Finningley. Following the closure of the latter base, both units are to be relocated within the RAF structure, and likewise Red Arrows will also vacate their home base at Scampton, which is also due to close.

The outstanding Hawk design has enjoyed considerable overseas sales success and a number of export versions have been produced, all based on the same airframe, albeit with minor systems changes or powerplant variations. Hawks have been exported to countries such as Finland, Indonesia, Kenya, Saudi Arabia, United Arab Emirates, Zimbabwe and Switzerland, and the type was successfully adopted by the United States Navy as a replacement for its fleet of T-2 Buckeye and TA-4 Skyhawks. Designated T-45 Goshawk, this navalised variant (produced in co-operation with McDonnell Douglas) is a radically redesigned version of the basic Hawk airframe, with strengthened undercarriage (including a twin-wheel nose gear), arrestor hook, twin airbrakes and improved powerplant.

OPPOSITE BELOW:
After disbanding in September 1992, No. 74 Squadron re-formed as No. 74(R) Squadron at RAF Valley, as part of No. 4 Flying Training School. The unit is equipped with Hawk advanced trainers, and one aircraft (*XX226*) keeps the spirit of 'Tigers' alive, thanks to this beautiful all-black paint scheme complete with a huge tiger emblem on the tail. It was planned to continue the tiger's body and tail right across the Hawk's fuselage, but the 'authorities' didn't approve the idea!
(Tim Laming)

BELOW:
As part of the RAF Advanced Flying Training syllabus, the Hawk is used to teach students the basic concepts of air defence fighter operations, and No. 74(R) Squadron's aircraft regularly fly air combat manoeuvring sorties. This stomach-churning picture shows the view from the Hawk's rear seat, as seen through the canopy MDC (miniature detonating cord). The lead Hawk has flipped over and is about to begin a sharp pull downwards into a half-loop, with the photo-ship 'interceptor' about to follow. *(Tim Laming)*

Further development of the Hawk continues, with the single-seat Hawk 200, optimised for tactical missions, and the first export deliveries having recently been made. The Hawk has proved to be a superb design in terms of reliability, manoeuvrability and 'pilot-friendliness', capable of undertaking a variety of roles including fighter, bomber all-weather attack, reconnaissance, anti-shipping strike, interdictor close air support, test and research vehicle, advanced trainer and weapons trainer, as well as being an outstanding formation aerobatics platform. Export sales continue to grow and the Hawk looks set to remain within the Royal Air Force inventory for many years to come. During 1994 the Hawk also entered service with the Royal Navy, replacing Hunters with the Fleet Requirements and Air Direction Unit at Yeovilton (eventually moving to Culdrose), flying 'aggressor' missions against land- and sea-based defence installations.

RIGHT:
Two Hawks break to starboard over North Wales, at the beginning of an advanced flying training exercise. The demanding course takes students directly from BFTS (Basic Flying Training School) through an advanced course (which includes high-speed navigation, formation flying and instrument flying), and into an applied phase which incorporates a variety of air-to-ground weapons delivery sorties and air-to-air combat missions, giving the students a basic capability in both roles.
(Tim Laming)

BELOW:
Returning at low level back to RAF Valley, two Hawks streak through the Welsh countryside after completing an air combat manoeuvring 'hop'. The Hawks were painted in this high-visibility colour scheme until recently, when overall grey camouflage was introduced. Some aircraft are appearing in an all-black scheme as, perhaps surprisingly, an all-black paint scheme appears to give the aircraft high conspicuity, an important safety factor.
(Tim Laming)

Sweeping over the Devon coastline, a pair of Hawk T1As from Nos. 151 (foreground) and 63 Squadrons, carrying a standard air defence weapons fit for the Hawk, a pair of AIM-9L Sidewinders and a single Aden cannon on the centreline. In addition to flying ACM sorties as part of the training syllabus, the Hawks are also assigned to a reserve wartime role as visual air defence fighters, working in co-operation with Tornado F3s on local air defence duties.
(British Aerospace)

ABOVE LEFT:
A long instrument approach to RAF Valley as seen from the Hawk's rear cockpit. The runway lights can be seen some miles ahead of the aircraft, offset to port. The aircraft is flying along the extended runway centreline and glidepath, but a strong crosswind is causing the aircraft to 'crab' quite markedly to starboard.
(Tim Laming)

ABOVE RIGHT:
Moving closer to the runway threshold, the Hawk's nose is slowly edging back towards the centreline. The Hawk's weapons-aiming gunsight is fairly basic, but provides the student and instructor with an effective means of aiming the Hawk's cannon, practice bombs and Sidewinder training rounds. This picture also emphasises the excellent all-round view available to the instructor, who normally occupies the rear seat. *(Tim Laming)*

RIGHT:
Almost at the runway threshold, the Hawk streaks over the perimeter road, shortly before touching down on the 'piano keys'. A precise approach is necessary, as Valley's secondary runway isn't particularly long, and on a wet day such as this every inch of concrete (and some careful brake application) is required if you're hoping to avoid rolling off the end of the runway into the sea! *(Tim Laming)*

LEFT:
Hawk T1A *XX247* 'CM' of No. 100 Squadron, climbing in formation with Canberra TT18 *WJ862* 'CU', also from No. 100 Squadron, pictured during the squadron's transition from the Canberra to the Hawk. Clearly visible under the Canberra's port wing is the hardpoint from which the Rushton target winch could be attached when required. For passive 'silent' sorties the winch packs were often removed in order to reduce drag, giving the aircraft additional manoeuvrability and range, and also reducing unnecessary fatigue on the airframe. *(British Aerospace)*

BELOW:
A very unusual photograph of a Hawk from No. 63 Squadron keeping formation with a banner target, being towed by a Canberra (out of picture). As can just be seen, the target is peppered with holes created by the Hawk's cannon shells. The holes are coloured blue, thanks to a range of dyes which are applied to the cannon shells, allowing more than one aircraft to fire at the same target, whilst still being able to identify which ammunition was fired by which pilot. *(British Aerospace)*

LOCKHEED HERCULES

The Royal Air Force was one of the first overseas customers for the Lockheed Hercules, a total of sixty-six C-130K variants being purchased, the first of which was delivered in September 1966. The C-130K is essentially a C-130H as operated by the USAF, but fitted with British avionics. Designed as a versatile tactical transport, the Hercules is capable of operating from semi-prepared airstrips and can operate over long distances whenever necessary through the use of air-to-air refuelling. The Hercules was heavily committed to transport operations during the 1982 Falklands conflict, and the aircraft was similarly employed during Operation 'Granby' 'Desert Storm'. More recently the RAF Hercules fleet has been heavily committed to relief flights in the former Yugoslavia, Rwanda and elsewhere.

The Hercules C1P is the standard RAF C-130 variant, fitted with a crude aerial refuelling system 'bolted on' to the upper fuselage (the refuelling probes were taken from retired Vulcans) which was rapidly constructed during the Falklands conflict. Some aircraft are now equipped with AN/ALQ-157 infra-red jammers and most are now fitted with AN/APN-169B station-keeping equipment. The Hercules C1K is a modified version employed as an aerial refuelling tanker, fitted with fuel tanks (in the cargo hold), used primarily in the Falklands. The refuelling hose drum unit is attached to the cargo door and Racal 'Orange Blossom' ECM equipment is fitted to the tanker's wingtips. Six aircraft were modified to tanker configuration although most are expected to be restored to the transport role.

OPPOSITE:
Although no longer in regular US Navy service, the Lockheed DC-130 Hercules still provides the Navy with a valuable service, acting as a launch and control platform for a variety of unmanned target drones. Former Navy aircraft are now operated by Tracor Flight Systems, based at Mojave airport, on behalf of the NAWC/WD at Point Mugu. *(Scott Van Aken)*

BELOW:
The Herky Bird also plays its part in the world of 'aggressor' operations. Lockheed's EC-130E and EC-130H are specialist electronic warfare aircraft, also assigned to signals intelligence gathering duties. Some aircraft are also equipped for communications jamming operations and, unlike many Hercules variants, the EC-130s are equipped for in-flight refuelling, as illustrated by this two-tone grey example taking on fuel from a KC-10 over the Californian desert during a 'Red Flag' exercise. *(Curtiss Knowles)*

The C3P is a 'stretched' derivative of the standard Hercules, incorporating two fuselage 'plugs' which lengthen the aircraft by some fifteen feet, thus increasing the aircraft's cargo-carrying capacity without requiring the additional cost of a second aircraft. Like the C1s, these aircraft have been progressively fitted with in-flight refuelling probes and associated fuel systems.

The Hercules W2, of which only one example was produced, is a specialised variant dedicated to weather research, and is currently operated by the Meteorological Research Flight, formerly based at Farnborough but relocated to Boscombe Down during 1994. Fitted with a variety of sensor equipment, the Hercules W2 is instantly recognisable thanks to a huge nose boom carrying air sensors, and a relocated weather radar housed in a pod above the flight deck. The Hercules fleet is due for replacement, and the RAF is keen to adopt a new Hercules C-130J variant, although politics prompted the Government to opt for both the C-130J and the European Future Large Aircraft, in whatever form it may finally fly.

MCDONNELL DOUGLAS F/A-18 HORNET

During the early 1970s the United States Department of Defense had anticipated that the US Navy would obtain a navalised version of the USAF's LWF (Light Weight Fighter), as a supplement to the existing fleet of F-14 Tomcats and A-7 Corsairs. The LWF, which later became the F-16, was a single-engined aircraft which the US Navy became increasingly uncomfortable with; it eventually opted to purchase a derivative of the twin-engine YF-17 Cobra which had lost to the F-16 in the LWF competition.

The YF-17 Cobra made its first flight on 9 June 1974 and McDonnell Douglas eventually emerged as prime contractor for production of the operational version of the aircraft, designated F-18A Hornet. Northrop remained involved with the programme, undertaking thirty per cent of the airframe development and forty per cent of airframe production, while General Electric would provide the powerplants in the shape of F404 low-bypass turbofans, developing 16,000 lb thrust. During the development process, the wing area was increased, a more robust landing gear was produced, wing-fold mechanisms were introduced, increased fuel capacity, an in-flight refuelling probe and provision for AIM-7 Sparrow AAMs.

Full-scale production began in January 1976 and the prototype F-18A made its first flight on 18 November 1978. Some 371 examples of the F-18A (later confirmed as having been designated F/A-18A) were produced for the USN and USMC before production switched to the F/A-18C with revised avionics and compatibility with

More impersonations: not a trio of MiGs, but three F/A-18A Hornets from VFA-127, racing over the Nevada desert. Careful application of colours and demarcation lines enables the Hornet to masquerade as a MiG-29, complete with fake insignia and imitation intake grilles on the wind LERXs. They might be easy to recognise as Hornets in this picture, but during an all-out aerial combat mission the effect can be quite convincing. *(Tom Walczyk)*

OPPOSITE TOP:
A closer look at the Hornet's underside reveals more details of how VFA-127 has disguised its aircraft as MiG-29s. Careful applications of light grey paint to the wing leading edges and tail section help to 'blot out' the Hornet's true planform, and the black diagonal line on the forward fuselage represents the 'Fulcrum's' intake position. Clever stuff, huh?! *(Tom Walczyk)*

BELOW:
VFA-203, the 'Blue Dolphins', based at Cecil Field in Florida, is a Naval Air Reserve unit primarily assigned to attack duties. However, the unit has recently acquired a secondary aggressor task, and a number of their Hornets have been repainted in representative 'MiG' paint schemes, as illustrated by F/A-18A *161926*. The light/dark grey camouflage doesn't seem particularly relevant to any MiG operator, but the paint demarcation lines and details give the aircraft a fairly convincing 'Fulcrum' outline.
(Scott Van Aken)

AIM-120 and IR Maverick missiles. A total of 355 aircraft were manufactured for the USN and USMC. The F/A-18B and F/A-18D are tandem-seat dual-control variants of the 'Alpha' and 'Charlie' models respectively. The Hornet features a built-in 20mm cannon and a total of nine weapons stations capable of carrying two AIM-9L/M Sidewinder AAMs, AIM-7F/Ms, sensor pods, AIM-120s, AGM-62 Walleyes, AGM-84 Harpoons, AGM-88 HARMs, nuclear weapons, GBU-10, 12 and 16 laser-guided bombs, ADM-141 TALDs, LAU-10s and much more. The immensely versatile Hornet is assigned to combat air patrol, forward air control, anti-ship, and many other missions. Used extensively by the USN and USMC during Operation 'Desert Storm' the Hornet looks set to enjoy a long and successful career, with new improved versions of the aircraft already under development. Export sales have also been successful, with Hornets already having been delivered to countries such as Canada, Spain and Australia. The Hornet also equips the world famous 'Blue Angels' United States Navy Demonstration Squadron based at Pensacola NAS in Florida.

RIGHT:
Over at Lemoore in California, VFA-303, the 'Goldenhawks', have also acquired a secondary dissimilar air combat role, and have painted some of their Hornets accordingly. The grey/grey scheme seems to have been widely adopted, although a grey/green scheme has also been seen; however the basic 'MiG' outline modifications are common to VFA-203, VFA-303 and VFA-127. F/A-18A *161710* demonstrates a capability that most 'Fulcrums' certainly don't possess: folding wings! *(Ted Carlson)*

BELOW:
Unusual underside view of a VAQ-34 Hornet, with what appears to be an AGM-84 Harpoon simulator round attached to the port wing pylon. The unit's markings were, to say the least, very restrained. Pictured on approach to Miramar NAS, the wingtip vortices suggest that the moist sea air has drifted inland from nearby San Diego. *(Tim Laming)*

Illustrating the concept of multi-national training, a Canadian Armed Forces CF-18 formates with a Belgian Air Force F-16, after completing an air combat mission over Germany. Without a dedicated dissimilar air combat 'aggressor' unit, NATO forces are now obliged to rely upon this kind of co-operation to provide fighter pilots with fairly realistic air combat training. *(Belgian Air Force)*

BELL UH-1

The United States Army issued a requirement for a casualty evacuation (casevac) and utility helicopter during the early 1950s, resulting in the Bell Model 204 which flew for the first time on 22 October 1956. Powered by an 825 shp Lycoming XT53-L-1 engine, it was the first turbine-powered aircraft to be adopted by the US Army. Six YH-40 helicopters were constructed for trials, and when the type was ordered into production it was given the designation HU-1A, prompting the famous 'Huey' name which has stayed with the helicopter throughout its career, despite being officially named 'Iroquois'.

The initial production version was the HU-1A, accommodating a crew of two plus six passengers or two stretchers. The HU-1B followed, with capacity for seven passengers or three stretchers. The UH-1C featured wide-chord rotor blades, giving better performance and a variety of sub-types followed, including the UH-1E for the United States Marine Corps, UH-1F and TH-1F for the United States Air Force, HH-1K for the United States Navy and the UH-1M for the US Army, fitted with night sensor equipment. Export sales were substantial, the Bell Model 204B being sold to countries such as Austria, Indonesia, South Korea, Malta, Norway, Sweden, Turkey and Venezuela. The type was also licence-built by Agusta in Italy (Agusta-Bell AB.204) and by Fuji in Japan (Fuji-Bell 204B-2).

Some 2,500 Model 204s were constructed for the US Armed Forces, and Bell developed the basic design still further, producing the Bell Model 205 which first flew on 16 August 1961. Ordered into production for the US Army under the designation UH-1D, more than 2,000 examples were constructed for the latter service. The UH-1D featured a lengthened fuselage (accommodating up to fourteen troops or six stretchers) and additional fuel capacity, while still retaining the earlier model's Lycoming T53-L-11 turboshaft engine.

Various sub-types of the Model 205 were produced such as the UH-1H (with increased power), CUH-1H for the Canadian Armed Forces (who redesignated the type CH-118), and HH-1H for the USAF. More than 3,500 UH-1H models were produced for the US Army and the helicopter looks set to remain in service well into the next century. Licence production in Italy and Japan and export models were also produced by Dornier in Germany and AIDC in Taiwan. Overseas customers comprise more than thirty countries, including Tunisia, Spain, Ecuador, Libya, Pakistan, Indonesia, Peru, Australia, Chile, Brazil, Burma, Bolivia, Singapore, Israel, New Zealand, Turkey and Vietnam.

ABOVE:
Not a Russian Hind, but a suitably camouflaged UH-1 Huey, operated by the United States Army in support of the National Training Center at Fort Irwin in California. The colour scheme and nose section give ground troops a fairly convincing image of the Hind, although the rapidly thawing relations between East and West may mean that the US Army eventually obtains *real* Hinds!
(Boudewijn Pieters)

OPPOSITE:
Vintage shot of two vintage jets. The Fleet Requirements and Air Direction Unit at Yeovilton continued to operate the Hunter until 1995 in support of various exercises, often acting as a representative hostile aggressor for ships' radar operators. British Aerospace Hawks have slowly been introduced into FRADU service and the Hunter's days with the Fleet Air Arm are now over. This nostalgic 1980s-vintage shot illustrates a pair of Hunter GA11s wearing what was for many years the standard Navy Hunter colour scheme, with dark grey upper surfaces, white undersides and full colour insignia. *(FAA)*

BRITISH AEROSPACE HUNTER

The Hawker Hunter became famous as a classic fighter design, destined to serve with the Royal Air Force for more than thirty years, enjoying export successes around the world. Entering service in 1954 (after making a first flight in July 1951), the Hunter F1 featured a powerful Rolls-Royce Avon engine, four internally housed Aden cannon, and an excellent stores carriage capability. The F4 and F6 developed the design still further through a series of powerplant improvements and aerodynamic modifications, culminating in what became the 'standard' Hunter, the FGA9, which formed the basis of many export versions.

A total of 1,927 Hunters were manufactured and approximately a third of this total are still active with various military air arms (and civilian operators) around the world. Many early Hunter variants were modified to FGA9 standard by British Aerospace, extending their capabilities and airframe life still further.

The twin-seat trainer version of the Hunter (the T7) was a relatively straightforward revision of the F4 airframe, with a side-by-side cockpit layout, originally housed under a twin-bubble canopy, which was later changed (prior to production) to the familiar one-piece hood. The only other major change was a corresponding increase in the length of the nose section and the fuselage spine, although the Aden cannon was refitted in bolt-on blisters, the port pod often being omitted. Some seventy-three Hunter T7s were delivered to the RAF (including single-seat rebuilds) and a further forty-five aircraft were manufactured (or converted) for the Royal Navy to T8 standard, with navalised equipment including a tail-mounted arrestor hook.

The Hunter was withdrawn from fighter and ground attack service by the end of the 1970s, and the remaining RAF fleet was assigned to tactical weapons training. Many aircraft were assigned to test flying and development work with the Ministry of Defence Procurement Executive and with British Aerospace. Large numbers of export Hunters have remained operational throughout the 1980s and 1990s, although the largest operator (Switzerland) withdrew the type during 1994, leaving only modest numbers of Hunters in service around the world. RAF Hunter operations effectively ended when the Buccaneer was withdrawn from service, the Hunter having been retained for twin-seat conversion training for the Buccaneer, for which a dual-control variant was never constructed. The Royal Navy's association with the Hunter ended in 1995 when the type was withdrawn from service with the Fleet Requirements and Air Direction Unit at Yeovilton, following delivery of former RAF Hawks.

Training new Buccaneer pilots presented the RAF with an unusual problem: no dual-control versions of the Buccaneer were ever produced, and so Hunter aircraft were fitted with Buccaneer instrumentation, and used for initial conversion on to type. However, the first 'solo' on the Buccaneer was always an attention-grabbing experience! The Hunters were also used as 'bounce' aircraft, a sort of informal 'aggressor', attacking Buccaneer formations to keep the 'Brick' pilots alert at all times. Towards the end of their career (the Hunters retired with the Buccaneers), some aircraft were repainted in an all-black paint scheme, recalling the days when the 'Black Arrows' delighted airshow crowds with their precision Hunter formation aerobatics.
(Tim Laming)

ABOVE:
The nostalgic sight of vintage jets, still working hard as part of the Fleet Requirements & Air Direction Unit (FRADU), based at Yeovilton in Somerset. The Hunter is an aged thoroughbred, loved by pilots and ground engineers. It's a fast, fairly agile and relatively inexpensive aircraft to operate, and FRADU employs the aircraft as a passive target for radar operator training, and weapons system operator training. *(Tim Laming)*

LEFT:
Although the Hunters wear Royal Navy markings, both the Hunter and Falcon 20 were civilian-operated, the Hunters being maintained and flown by Airwork Ltd. Most FRADU Hunter missions are flown directly from home base at Yeovilton (the majority of the exercises taking place over the English Channel), although aircraft do occasionally deploy to Sardinia and Gibraltar. *(Peter Foster)*

ABOVE:
The Falcon 20 and Hunter 'package' presents radar operators with a convincing threat simulation. On the radar screen, the Falcon 20 represents a hostile attack aircraft, while the Hunter simulates a sea-skimming missile. The Hunter's dark grey camouflage is particularly effective at low level over the sea, where the FRADU aircraft spend much of their time. The Falcons, by contrast, wear high-visibility colours, largely as a safety consideration. (Tim Laming)

RIGHT:
After successfully 'launching' from their Falcon 20 mother ship, the Hunters descend to ultra-low level (and I do mean *low*!), and accelerate towards their target. On the radar screen, the Hunter looks and acts like an Exocet-class missile, breaking away just short of the anticipated impact point, roaring overhead the darkened radar room. As seen from this Hunter (in a post-attack climb), this German warship had entered a tight defensive turn in response to the Hunter attack. The FRADU Hunters' pilots fly up to 400 hours each year, making this civilian job an attractive option for any former RAF/FAA fast-jet pilot. (Tim Laming)

SEPECAT JAGUAR

The defence ministries of Great Britain and France initiated the Jaguar project during 1975, a company named SEPECAT (Société Européenne de Production de l'Avion ECAT) being formed to manage the project. Although the Jaguar began life as an advanced trainer, the design was (largely due to RAF requirements) developed into a very capable ground attack aircraft. The first example, a twin-seat trainer, made its first flight on 8 September 1968 and deliveries to the RAF began in 1973, ending in 1978. Although the Jaguar was expected to be withdrawn during the early 1990s, the Ministry of Defence decided to retain the aircraft beyond the year 2000, although a more recent airpower study suggests that the Jaguar's withdrawal may occur at an earlier date.

The Jaguar GR1A is a single-seat, low-level ground attack aircraft which replaced the Phantom in the interdiction and counter-air role. Delivered with Adour Mk 102 turbofans rated at 7,305 lb thrust, the RAF Jaguar fleet was retrofitted with uprated Adour Mk 104 engines, rated at 8,040 lb thrust during the 1978–1984 period. The GR1 was modified to GR1A standard when the original inertial navigation system was replaced by a Ferranti FIN 1064 system. Weapons include 1,000 lb free-fall and retarded bombs. Paveway laser-guided bombs, CBU-87 cluster bombs, BL.755 cluster bombs and nineteen-round LAU-500B/A pods of CRV.7 rockets. AIM-9L Sidewinder AAMs can be carried, normally on overwing missile rails, and self-protection equipment

Racing over the North Yorkshire moors, a Royal Air Force Jaguar GR1A heads for the Spadeadam weapons range during an exercise in 1992. The RAF currently operates three Jaguar squadrons (Nos. 6, 41 and 54) based at Coltishall in Norfolk, together with an Operational Conversion Unit at Lossiemouth, recently re-designated as No. 16(R) Squadron.
(Tim Laming)

From the rear seat of a Jaguar T2A, the lead aircraft can be seen thundering over the Yorkshire moorland, during a low-level attack on radar units at Spadeadam in Cumbria. The head-up display registers a speed of 420 knots and a height of 355 feet, a figure which varies wildly as the radar altimeter compensates for the undulating landscape below. Forward vision from the Jaguar's rear seat isn't fantastic, but it's adequate for conversion training tasks, and peripheral vision is superb. *(Tim Laming)*

also includes a Phimat chaff/flare dispenser and an ALQ-101 ECM pod. Radar Warning Receivers are also attached to the GR1A's tail.

The Jaguar GR1A is also operated in the reconnaissance role by No. 41 Squadron based at Coltishall. A centreline-mounted BAe reconnaissance pod is carried for this task, containing five Vinten F.95 cameras together with a vertical infra-red linescan camera, although this equipment can be substituted by an F.126 survey camera (as during the Gulf War). The reconnaissance-configured Jaguar remains fully combat-capable and retains the internally mounted pair of 30mm Aden cannon, each with 180 rounds of ammunition. Jaguars have also been progressively fitted with ALE-40 ECM equipment, attached to the lower rear fuselage.

The Jaguar T2A is a tandem-seat dual-control trainer version of the Jaguar, retaining a similar combat capability. Most T2As are operated by the Jaguar Operational Conversion Unit at Lossiemouth, although a pair of twin-seaters is normally attached to each of the three operational RAF Jaguar squadrons for continuation training.

LEFT:
Low over the Norfolk countryside, a Jaguar GR1A reveals her armament fit comprising a centreline-mounted laser-guided bomb, internally mounted cannon, and two AIM-9L Sidewinder AAMs, giving the aircraft a very effective self-protection capability (Sidewinder rails have more recently been fitted over the Jaguar's wing upper surfaces). The Jaguar is a fairly agile aircraft, and more than capable of 'holding her own' in a fight with a marauding interceptor. *(British Aerospace)*

BELOW:
Unusual oblique view of a Jaguar GR1A, this particular machine wearing special markings to celebrate No. 54 Squadron's seventy-fifth anniversary. Jaguars regularly participate in many RAF and NATO exercises, even occasionally still venturing as far afield as Nellis AFB to participate in 'Red Flag' exercises. *(British Aerospace)*

BOEING KC-135 STRATOTANKER

Developed from the world famous Boeing Model 367-80 demonstrator (which was transformed into the classic Boeing 707 airliner design), the first KC-135A Stratotanker made its maiden flight on 31 August 1956, the first of 732 aircraft being delivered to the USAF's Strategic Air Command (at Castle AFB in California) during June 1957. The KC-135A was generally similar to the 'Dash-80' in layout, although the Stratotanker and Boeing 707 were developed as two distinctly separate programmes, resulting in two very different airframes.

Minor modifications to the design were made following entry into USAF service, most notably the extension of the tail-fin (giving the aircraft greater yaw stability) and the addition of 'straps' to the rear fuselage to prevent fuselage cracking caused by jet engine shock waves. The aircraft was, however, extremely successful, as was the (then) new 'flying boom' refuelling system which was also developed by Boeing. In addition to refuelling tanker duties (primarily in support of SAC B-47 and B-52 bombers), the KC-135 was also operated as a strategic transport thanks to the capacious cabin structure and a large cargo door in the port fuselage wall. Up to eighty passengers could also be carried if necessary.

The KC-135A was powered by four Pratt & Whitney J57-59W turbojets each of which developed 13,750 lb thrust. During the 1980s the USAF embarked upon a re-engining programme for much of the Stratotanker fleet, replacing the uneconomical and environmentally unfriendly turbojets with JT3D turbofans taken from redundant Boeing 707 airframes (the engines were given the military TF33 designation). Tail units, engine pylons and cowlings were also taken from airliners, and having already been the subject of a fatigue extension programme, these 'new' tankers were redesignated KC-135E, most being assigned to Air National Guard and AFRES units.

The remainder of the KC-135 fleet was also upgraded in a more dramatic form, the J57s being replaced by CFM International CFM56 (military designation F108) high bypass ratio turbofans, each developing a staggering 22,000 lb thrust. Auxiliary power units were also fitted, giving the aircraft a self-start capability and, with a greater fuel capacity, the KC-135R represents a leap in technology over the original KC-135A model. Both the 'E' and 'R' models look set to remain in the USAF inventory well into the next century, as well as a bewildering variety of 135 variants assigned to various missions.

SAAB J32 LANSEN

Despite being a very able jet-powered attack aircraft, the Lansen's design history dates back as far as the mid-1940s, when the Royal Swedish Air Force first issued a requirement for a new twin-seat all-weather attack aircraft. Saab proposed the R119 powered by a pair of de Havilland Ghost turbojets, but the design was rejected late in 1948 on the grounds of complexity and relatively high cost. An alternative proposal was submitted and adopted shortly afterwards, resulting in four prototype Saab 32s, the first aircraft making its maiden flight on 3 November 1952.

Powered by a single (imported) Rolls-Royce Avon turbojet, the Saab 32 was a conventional design of metal construction, with hydraulically boosted aileron controls, an all-moving tailplane and a pressurised cockpit for pilot and observer. Production aircraft featured Swedish-built versions of the Rolls-Royce Avon engine, fitted with a Swedish-developed afterburner unit. Production began in 1953 and the first A32A Lansen (Lance) joined Flygflottilj 17 during December 1955. Fitted with four 20mm cannon and hardpoints for bombs, rockets or RB04 anti-ship missiles, the A32A was an unqualified success.

Development of the Lansen continued, resulting in the J32B with a more powerful Flygmotor RM6B (Avon 200) engine, developing 15,212 lb thrust. With 30mm cannon, Sidewinder AAMs and new navigation and fire control systems, the J32B first flew on 7 January 1957, entering service during the following year. The ultimate Lansen variant was the J32C developed for reconnaissance duties and equipped to carry a variety of camera equipment. Flying for the first time on 26 March 1957 (and entering service the following year) the J32C was later modified to carry a mix of camera and sensor equipment.

A total of 450 Lansens was constructed, and although the type has long since disappeared from active service as a ground attack aircraft, the Lansen remains active in small numbers as an electronic countermeasures platform (for training duties) and as a target tug. The remaining Lansens carry a variety of equipment ranging from photographic reconnaissance cameras to cloud-sampling sensor pods. Not surprisingly, Lansens were heavily involved in cloud sampling operations following the Chernobyl nuclear powerplant accident.

The Saab J32 Lansen is still active, flying with Sweden's Flygflottilj F13M at Malmstatt, albeit in small numbers. Long since retired from front-line service as a fighter and ground attack aircraft, the Lansen is utilised as an ECM trainer, with additional reconnaissance and air sampling capabilities. Lansen '04' was pictured during 1984, carrying an interesting array of ECM pods and antennae. *(Fritz Becker)*

BRITISH AEROSPACE LIGHTNING

Without doubt, the Lightning was the Royal Air Force's most famous post-war fighter, and earned the distinction of being the last in a long line of British-designed single-seat fighter and attack aircraft, and the only all-British supersonic aircraft to enter operational service. It was also the fastest aircraft ever to serve with the RAF and one which, despite some obvious shortcomings, was greatly respected by generations of RAF pilots. The English Electric P1B first flew during 1958, entering service as the Lightning with No. 74 Squadron in 1960. Unfortunately, early promise of long-term design development was curtailed following Government re-thinking which (mistakenly) believed that future air defence needs would be met by a variety of surface-to-air missiles.

Despite official opposition, the Lightning was developed, which resulted in the F1A, F2 and F3, followed by the F2A and F6 with greater fuel capacity, revised wing plan, more power and greater manoeuvrability. The T4 and T5 were twin-seat trainer derivatives of the F1 and F3 respectively with side-by-side seating. The greater fuel capacity of the F2A and F6 (through the addition of a huge belly tank) enabled the Lightning also to carry a pair of Aden 30mm cannon with 120 rounds of ammunition per gun. However, the main armament for the Lightning was a pair of Firestreak or Red Top infra-red air-to-air missiles which were carried on missile rails on the lower forward fuselage.

Export versions were produced for Kuwait and Saudi Arabia (Lightning F53) which were fitted with outboard wing hardpoints, enabling the aircraft to carry rocket pods or bombs for a limited ground attack capability. Uniquely, the Lightning F6 (and export versions) were also able to carry huge overwing fuel tanks, although these were rarely used in RAF service in order to maintain wing fatigue life. Fuel capacity was always a major concern for Lightning pilots, and the type's poor endurance was perhaps the Lightning's only vice. The Lightning was fitted with a crude bolt-on refuelling probe, but a more effective retractable probe was never developed, essentially because of the continuing belief that the aircraft would quickly become obsolete (although of course, it didn't). Likewise, plans to fit the aircraft with Sidewinder AAMs never proceeded beyond the concept phase.

A total of 338 Lightnings was produced, the last examples leaving RAF service in the 1980s. Following retirement, a handful of airframes continued to fly with British Aerospace as part of the Tornado F3's radar development programme. The Lightnings acted as high-speed targets for the Tornado until they became redundant in 1993.

BELOW:
A magnificent picture of three magnificent RAF interceptors, all wearing the markings of No. 56 Squadron, one of the Royal Air Force's most famous fighter units. This picture was taken as the unit transitioned from the Phantom to the Tornado F3, becoming No. 56(R) Squadron in the process. They were joined by British Aerospace's Lightning *XP693*, to make a delightful formation showing three fighter types which were operated by the unit. *(British Aerospace)*

RIGHT:
An unmistakable profile, the awesome Lightning F6 was finally retired from RAF service during 1988, marking the end of a long and successful RAF career. It was also the last in a long line of single-seat RAF fighters, breaking a long tradition which will not be restored until the Eurofighter enters RAF service. The Lightning was more than a match for anything other than a high-tech fighter, with a very capable pilot. *(Tim Laming)*

LEFT:
Following the retirement of the last RAF Lightnings, a small number of airframes were transferred to British Aerospace at Warton, where the aircraft were utilised as high-speed aerial targets in support of the continuing Tornado F3 radar development programme. Warton was an appropriate base for the Lightnings, as they had been built there a quarter of a century previously. When the Tornado radar programme ended, the Lightnings were withdrawn, but plans are being made to fly Lightnings as 'warbirds', providing that the ever-cautious Civil Aviation Authority can be persuaded to sanction these plans.
(Tim Laming)

GLOSTER METEOR

The Gloster Meteor has earned an important place in the history of aviation as the first jet-powered aircraft to enter operational service, anywhere in the world. Although an unremarkable aircraft by modern standards, the Meteor was a truly revolutionary design, making the technical leap from propeller-driven combat aircraft to the new era of turbine power. Although initially little more than an experimental design, the Meteor became the Royal Air Force's primary fighter aircraft, equipping dozens of squadrons both in the UK and overseas. The aircraft was also a successful export product, and has soldiered on in various forms until the present day, when two aircraft are still in operational use, some fifty years since the type first entered RAF service.

Following the first flight of Gloster's E28/39 experimental jet-powered aircraft from Cranwell on 15 May 1941, the Royal Air Force was already awaiting development of an operational jet fighter based around specification F9/40 issued by the Air Ministry. It was accepted that an aircraft could not be designed around a single jet engine, and so a twin-engined design was established, and an order for twelve aircraft was issued to Gloster Aircraft on 7 February 1941. In fact, only eight of these aircraft were actually built, and it was the fifth airframe which made the type's first flight from Cranwell on 5 March 1943. Interestingly, this flight was made without Frank Whittle's engine as delays in completing production-standard engines (by Rover Motors) led to the use of de Havilland Halford H1 powerplants for this first air test flight.

Air Ministry disinterest in jet power was suddenly transformed into optimism, and in June 1941 Glosters received an order for 300 aircraft to the F9/40 specifications, the name 'Meteor' being selected in February 1942. The Rover W2B engine was named 'Welland'. The first Meteors to enter service joined No. 616 Squadron at Culmhead on 21 July 1944, moving to a forward base at Manston shortly afterwards. The unit's primary task was the interception of German V-1 flying bombs, and the first Meteor 'kill' took place on 4 August when a V-1 was destroyed by flipping the weapon into a dive (the Meteor's machine-guns having failed to fire). The Meteor was developed into more manoeuvrable and powerful versions, the F8 becoming the 'standard' RAF fighter variant, followed by a series of night-fighter variants and a variety of export versions supplied to countries such as France, Egypt, the Netherlands, Belgium, Brazil, Denmark, Israel and Australia. Although long since withdrawn from widespread operational use, a pair of Meteor D16 manned/unmanned target drones remains active with the Defence Research Agency at Llanbedr, although they are likely to be withdrawn shortly, following delivery of suitably modified Hawk aircraft.

LEFT:
The DRA at Llanbedr operates a single Meteor as a 'shepherd' for their fleet of Jindivik target drones, which are regularly used as targets for RAF fighter pilots flying from RAF Valley on live missile firing sorties. The Meteor can also be flown as a target, although every attempt is made to keep the Meteor intact, at least for the time being, until a Hawk is modified to undertake the same role. What will then happen to this venerable fighter remains unclear, but it is to be hoped that she doesn't make a one-way trip for an appointment with a Sidewinder!
(Tim Laming)

ABOVE:
VZ467 was the Royal Air Force's last operational Meteor, serving as a banner target tug with No. 1 Tactical Weapons Unit at RAF Brawdy, before earning an honourable retirement. The Meteor was flown in support of the co-located Hawk units, which flew air combat manoeuvring sorties with the Meteor, firing their centreline-mounted cannon against a hessian banner towed by the Meteor. Following some years in storage, *VZ467* is about to return to the air as a civilian-owned warbird. *(Tim Laming)*

DASSAULT-BREGUET MIRAGE F1C

Although the Mirage F1 might be regarded as a relatively modern design, its developmental history can be traced back to the mid-1960s, when Dassault produced a single-engined version of its huge twin-engined Mirage F2 design (itself derived from the abortive Anglo-French Variable-Geometry aircraft project). Suitably scaled down and powered by a single Atar engine, the Mirage F1 flew for the first time on 23 December 1966. Unlike its famous delta-winged Mirage III counterpart, the Mirage F1 featured a more conventional wing and tailplane layout which, despite being smaller in terms of gross area, delivered much greater aerodynamic efficiency, thanks to the incorporation of full-span leading edge slats and double-slotted trailing edge flaps.

Internal fuel capacity in the Mirage F1 was also greatly improved over the Mirage III (from 646 to 946 imp. gal.) and most of the Mirage F1C fleet delivered to the Armée de l'Air were fitted with bolt-on refuelling probes to increase range still further. The first production Mirage F1C took to the air in February 1973 and was delivered to the French Air Force one month later, the first F1C unit being the 30ème Escadre de Chasse at Reims.

In addition to tandem twin-seat trainer derivatives, a number of export versions of the Mirage F1 have also been produced. These include the Mirage F1A, which is a simplified version of the F1C with a smaller, less capable radar, assigned primarily to daylight visual attack missions. Libya and South Africa purchased the type, the latter country possessing licence to build the aircraft (SAAF aircraft are designated Mirage F1AZ). Dassault-Breguet also developed an improved version of the F1C, designated Mirage F1E, with an uprated powerplant and improved avionics. Intended for NATO procurement, the type was not adopted and Dassault reassigned the designation to its Mirage F1 export version which has been sold to a variety of countries including Ecuador, Iraq, Jordan, Morocco, Qatar and Spain.

Although the Mirage F1E can be assigned to the reconnaissance role (through the attachment of various under-fuselage equipment), a purpose-designed reconnaissance variant of the Mirage F1 was not produced until the 1980s, when the first Mirage F1CR made its maiden flight in November 1981. Equipped with optical camera systems and sideways-looking radar, the Mirage F1CR is optimised for low- or high-level high-speed (Mach 1) reconnaissance and has replaced the Mirage IIIR within the Armée de l'Air.

ABOVE:
France's Armée de l'Air is, of course, a major European military air arm, although it remains outside the formal NATO structure. Despite this semi-isolationist position, the AdlA regularly participates in NATO exercises, and also participates in squadron exchanges with other NATO units. French fighters, such as this Mirage F-1C, regularly visit the UK flying air combat sorties with RAF Tornado F3 interceptors. *(AdlA)*

OPPOSITE TOP:
Swiss selection; although NATO forces are fairly well-documented, there are other European air arms which don't receive much publicity. Although Switzerland traditionally maintains a low-key and neutral military posture, the country possesses a formidable amount of military power, including a sizeable air force. Pictured during October 1988, two Mirage IIIS interceptors head out on a one-versus-one air combat sortie, taking turns to act as friendly and hostile fighters. *(Tim Laming)*

LOCKHEED P-3 ORION

Designed as a replacement for the Lockheed P-2 Neptune, Lockheed developed a new maritime reconnaissance and anti-submarine warfare aircraft from their L-188 Electra airliner. During May 1958 Lockheed was awarded a contract to develop their ASW aircraft design and converted the third Electra airframe into the prototype, installing a tail-mounted magnetic anomaly detector (MAD) boom and a ventral bulge to simulate a weapons bay. The fuselage was also shortened, and following a series of other minor modifications, the YP3V-1 made its first flight on 25 November 1959. Seven aircraft were duly ordered for the US Navy and in 1962 the aircraft was redesignated P-3 and named 'Orion'.

Entering service with VP-8 during 1962, some 157 P-3As were manufactured, followed by the P-3B, powered by uprated Allison T56-A-14 engines. Heavier than the A model, the P-3B was capable of carrying the AGM-12 Bullpup ASM. Norway and New Zealand became the first export customers for the Orion, each ordering five aircraft followed by Australia (ten aircraft). Production of the P-3B ended in 1969 and attention turned to the P-3C, a much-improved version of the Orion with new sensor systems and control equipment. Development continued, resulting in the P-3C Updates I to IV featuring the latest advances in anti-submarine sensor technology and maritime weapon development.

Export sales continued with six aircraft being supplied to Iran during 1975 (P-3F), their aircraft being unique in possessing an in-flight refuelling capability. The Netherlands, Japan, Spain and Portugal also acquired the Orion, and the aircraft continues to operate with each of the original customer countries as well as the United States Navy. Following the British Ministry of Defence's decision to seek a Nimrod replacement, the P-3 Orion has also become a serious contender for the Royal Air Force's future anti-submarine warfare needs, although British Aerospace are hoping to secure a contract to refurbish Nimrods, while France hopes to win the competition with Dassault-Breguet's Atlantic design.

The P-3 Orion has been modified to undertake various specialised duties, many aircraft being operated as test platforms with both military and civilian research units. One P-3A was converted to EP-3A standard as an electronic intelligence-gathering platform, being operated by the NATC and NWL at Patuxent River. Further aircraft were converted to EP-3B standard and others to EP-3E standard, entering operational service with VQ-1 and VQ-2. Packed with radar and communication sensor systems, the EP-3E is used primarily to collect and store radar and radio signals, enabling military analysts to determine the purpose and range of such emissions.

VAQ-33's current 'heavy' is the Lockheed EP-3 Orion, a highly capable electronic warfare and threat simulation platform. The Orion can simulate hostile reconnaissance and maritime patrol aircraft using sophisticated communications jamming equipment, as well as some 'low-tech' deception techniques such as chaff/flare dispensers. *(Tim Laming)*

PILATUS PC-9

The Pilatus PC-9 was, according to many informed commentators, 'the best trainer the Royal Air Force never had', it having lost a 1984-5 competition to replace the RAF's Jet Provost fleet, when the British Government opted to purchase Shorts (Embraer) Tucanos. It was no secret that the RAF wanted the PC-9, but political considerations led to the choice of the Tucano, not least because the aircraft was built in Northern Ireland where job creation was an important factor.

However, the PC-9 has enjoyed considerable sales success elsewhere, since making its first flight on 7 May 1984. Essentially a development of the early PC-7 design, the aircraft looks remarkably similar to its predecessor despite sharing only ten per cent commonality of structural components. Unlike the PC-7, the PC-9 features a larger 'stepped up' canopy, a four-blade propeller and twin ejection seats. The PT6A-62 turboprop engine delivers 1,150 hp in comparison with the PC-7's 650 hp, and the PC-9 is without doubt a considerable improvement over the earlier design, having earned a reputation as one of the best basic trainer types currently available.

As part of the competition to replace the RAF Jet Provost fleet (Air Staff Target 412), Pilatus teamed up with British Aerospace for marketing purposes. Following the conclusion of the AST 412 saga, the Pilatus/BAe team continued their sales efforts and quickly secured a deal with Saudi Arabia for the supply of thirty aircraft, which would be used for basic training prior to advanced training on Hawks (in much the same way as Pilatus/BAe had hoped the RAF system would have worked). Sales have continued, with Australia becoming another major operator of the type. Surprisingly, however, only a small number of PC-9s have so far entered service with the Swiss Air Force, the PC-7 remaining active as Switzerland's basic trainer type. A handful of PC-9s have joined the Swiss Air Force, however, as target facilities aircraft, having replaced a small fleet of obsolete Vampire trainers. It is likely that more PC-9s will eventually be purchased as the PC-7 fleet approaches withdrawal.

LEFT:
Switzerland was associated with the de Havilland Vampire until recently, when the last examples were finally withdrawn from service, and mostly sold to civilian operators. Amongst the last examples to serve with the Swiss Air Force were these brightly coloured target facilities aircraft, used to provide airborne targets for anti-aircraft gunners. Through an ingenious mirror targeting arrangement, the gunners were able to aim directly at the Vampire targets, whilst physically pointing their guns in the opposite direction. The diminutive Vampire wasn't powerful enough to tow a target. *(Tim Laming)*

BELOW:
Having retired the Vampire, a small number of Pilatus PC-9 turboprop trainers have been assigned to the target-towing role. This inexpensive turboprop is an ideal aircraft for both target-towing and 'silent' target flying (i.e. the aircraft acting as the target). By all accounts the PC-9 is an outstanding trainer design, and had British politicians not influenced the choice of replacement for the RAF's Jet Provost Fleet, the Royal Air Force would probably be flying the PC-9 rather than the Tucano. *(Tim Laming)*

MCDONNELL DOUGLAS F-4 PHANTOM

Perhaps the most famous post-WWII combat aircraft, the F-4 Phantom began life during 1953, the prototype XF4H-1 making its first flight in May 1953 leading to a three-year developmental programme and the delivery of the first F4H-1F Phantoms (later redesignated F-4A) to the US Navy in June 1961. The 'Alpha' model (which was essentially the same airframe as the earlier prototype) was quickly joined by the first fully operational variant, the F-4B, complete with a J79-GE-8A engine, modified cockpit and canopies, and an AN/APQ-72 radar. Deliveries to the USMC began a year later and at the same time the United States Air Force opted to purchase the Phantom, ordering the F-4C with APQ-100 radar, bombing radar and a missile system. The F-4C and the more capable F-4D saw extensive service during the Vietnam War, as did USN and USMC F-4Bs and F-4Js. The 'Juliet' model featured an improved radar, uprated engines, slatted leading edge tailplanes, additional fuel cells and many other improvements. The F-4B was developed into the RF-4B photo-reconnaissance platform for the USN and USMC (the RF-4C being a similar USAF derivative).

Later developments for the USN and USMC were converted from F-4B and F-4J models, resulting in the F-4N and F-4S, both being direct improvements of the earlier models with equipment upgrades and aerodynamic modifications. The USAF, however, acquired the F-4E, the most widely used Phantom variant, essentially redesigned around a huge multi-barrel 20mm cannon. The F-4E was widely used throughout the 1970s and 1980s both as a strike/attack aircraft and an air defence fighter, by regular USAF and ANG/AFRES units.

ABOVE:
A rare machine indeed, this EF-4J Phantom was operated by VAQ-33 in the electronic warfare aggressor role, acting as a 'threat simulator' training aid for radar operators. Although the aircraft is essentially an F-4J with additional electronic equipment, the 'EF' designation was approved by the US Navy in December 1976, and just two examples (*153076* and *153084*) entered service.
(Andy Hodgson collection)

RIGHT BOTTOM:
The distinctive profile of the legendary Phantom, pictured late in 1992 shortly before the Royal Air Force retired the last examples of the Phantom FGR2. The Phantom was the RAF's main interceptor type following the Lightning's withdrawal, and served with great distinction until being 'replaced' by the Tornado F3. Some would say that the Tornado interceptor wasn't much of a replacement for a classic dogfighter such as the Phantom, but the fact remains that the RAF is now without a true 'fighter' and will remain so until deliveries of the Eurofighter begin.
(Tim Laming)

LEFT:
Although the legendary Phantom has now been retired from front-line US Navy service, the F-4 lives on at China Lake and Point Mugu, where the NAWC/WD operate Phantoms as unmanned target drones, range safety patrol aircraft and airborne drone controllers. These QF-4N aircraft (converted F-4N airframes) have slowly taken over the target drone role from the QF-86 Sabre, and look set to remain in use for the foreseeable future. *(Scott Van Aken)*

The hugely successful Phantom was first exported in its F-4C form with examples being delivered to Iran, South Korea and Spain. F-4E derivatives were sold to Egypt, West Germany (F-4F), Greece, Iran, Israel, South Korea, Japan and Turkey. The type remains active with most of these export customers in both the ground attack and fighter roles. The Phantom was also exported to the United Kingdom, the F-4K and F-4M being redesigned versions of the F-4C and F-4D with British equipment, including Rolls-Royce Spey turbofan engines. Surplus USN/USMC F-4Js were also purchased for the RAF, although the entire Phantom fleet was withdrawn by the end of 1993.

The US Navy continues to operate the Phantom as the QF-4N, a sizeable fleet of former F-4N aircraft being used as unmanned target drones, gradually replacing the QF-86 Sabre at Point Mugu and China Lake as high-speed targets for missile development tasks.

ABOVE:
Following the end of the 1982 Falklands conflict, air defence forces were permanently stationed on the Falkland Islands, and No. 29 Squadron maintained a four-aircraft detachment on the islands until 1988, when the unit was re-numbered No. 1435 Flight. Supported by personnel on rotation from UK/Germany-based Phantom squadrons, the aircraft carried large Maltese cross motifs on their tails (No. 1435 Flight became famous as the WWII unit based in Malta with Gladiators) and carried the historically appropriate names (as applied to the Gladiators) *Faith*, *Hope*, *Charity* and *Despair*. Tornado F3s replaced the Phantoms in July 1992. *(Paul Jackson)*

RIGHT BOTTOM:
Once a famous RAF Lightning squadron, No. 74 Squadron reappeared in 1984, equipped with F-4J(UK) Phantoms purchased 'secondhand' from the US Navy and Marine Corps. The Phantoms were acquired in response to a perceived shortage of air defence assets, after Phantoms were deployed to the Falklands and deliveries of operational-standard Tornado F3s suffered continual delays. Fifteen aircraft were purchased at a cost of £33 million, and although F-14s and F-15s were considered, the MoD opted for Phantoms in an effort to maintain commonality with the Phantom fleet already in RAF service. In reality, the F-4J was almost a completely different aircraft. *(Tim Laming)*

LEFT:
Just what you don't want to see in your rear-view mirror, an ultra-close look at the Phantom FGR2, the pilot's face visible through the windscreen and head-up display panel. The F-4M's huge air intakes are also prominent, emphasising their increased size when compared to J-79-powered Phantom variants. The larger intakes supplied the increased airflow required by the Rolls-Royce Spey turbofans which, despite their greater thrust, gave the F-4M an inferior performance when compared to the F-4J, for example, thanks to a corresponding increase in airframe weight and drag.
(Tim Laming)

ABOVE:
Pictured en route to an exciting two-versus-two ACM sortie, three F-4Js take on fuel from a 216 Squadron Tristar over the North Sea, as seen from the cockpit of the fourth aircraft. No. 74 Squadron's Phantoms participated in many air defence exercises, as well as flying daily ACM sorties from home base at Wattisham as part of their regular training programme. Sadly, most of the F-4Js ended their days on fire dumps, although one aircraft did survive, and currently resides with the Imperial War Museum at Duxford.
(Tim Laming)

RIGHT:
Breaking away from the camera, an F-4J(UK) reveals the aircraft's undersides. Four AIM-9 Sidewinder missile rails are carried, although just one Sidewinder 'acquisition round' is fitted. Likewise, a similar Skyflash round is carried in the forward port bay, with the remaining three bays empty. The centreline hardpoint and outer wing hardpoints are also empty, and most of 74 Squadron's F-4J training sorties were flown in this configuration.
(Tim Laming)

GRUMMAN A-6 INTRUDER/EA-6B PROWLER

The Grumman A-6 Intruder design dates back to 1957 when the US Navy issued a requirement for an all-weather day/night attack aircraft. Eleven companies submitted proposals to meet this request and Grumman's G-128 was selected, a total of eight A2F-1 development aircraft being ordered and the first of these making its first flight on 19 April 1960. The functional lines of the A2F-1 (redesignated A-6A in 1962) reflect the rugged design of the airframe, combined with outstanding computer technology which made the aircraft into a superb strike/attack weapons platform. Just under 500 A-6A Intruders were manufactured, the last being delivered in 1969.

The A-6E which followed the 'Alpha' model represented a leap in technology, featuring a new multi-mode navigation and attack radar and other avionics improvements. It was later fitted with the TRAM (Target Recognition Attack Multi-sensor) system, giving the aircraft a FLIR (Forward-Looking Infra-Red) capability to deliver weapons with extreme accuracy in all weather conditions. The Intruder was developed into a small number of specialised variants, the A-6B being a SAM suppression variant, the A-6C a night attack type, and the KA-6D an in-flight refuelling tanker which remains active with the USN. The EA-6B was a specialised ECM (Electronic Countermeasures) platform

The EA-6A Intruder was the forerunner of the EA-6B Prowler, the Navy's dedicated electronic warfare platform. Less capable than the Prowler, and produced in relatively low numbers as a replacement for the EF-10B Skynight, the EA-6A soldiered on in very small numbers until the early nineties, this VAQ-33 example is seen at Miramar in 1993. *(Tim Laming)*

designed for the USMC which remained in service until the early 1990s. Although the A-6E remains fully operational with the US Navy, the type is no longer active with the USMC and further deliveries of F/A-18 Hornets will enable the USN to withdraw the Intruder by the end of the decade.

The EA-6B Prowler is a direct development of the Intruder airframe, designed to replace the EKA-3B Skywarrior ECM platform (the earlier, less sophisticated EA-6A was developed as a replacement for the USMC's EF-10B Skynight). Unlike the A-6, however, the Prowler features an extended fuselage and a second cockpit, housing an additional two-man crew, enabling three electronic warfare officers (designated ECMOs – Electronic Countermeasures Operators) to fly onboard the aircraft to manage the sophisticated array of ECM and ESM equipment carried by the aircraft. Flying for the first time in May 1968, the Prowler entered service in 1972, participating in the latter stages of the Vietnam War. Used as an intelligence-gathering platform, ECM escort (accompanying strike packages both to monitor enemy signals and to counter them with jamming signals), and as a stand-off ECM platform (orbiting at some distance, creating an electronic 'smoke screen'), the Prowler is also capable of carrying up to four AGM-88 HARM missiles.

ABOVE:
The Grumman EA-6B Prowler electronic countermeasures and anti-radar platform equips a large number of US Navy squadrons, concentrated at Whidbey Island in Washington. As a purpose-designed EW aircraft, the Prowler is regularly used as a representative hostile aircraft in many training exercises, flying radar and communications-jamming profiles. With an appropriately named pilot, this VAQ-35 machine was pictured at Miramar early in 1993. *(Tim Laming)*

OPPOSITE – TOP:
The North American QF-100 target drone programme was particularly successful, with over 300 conversions being made by Sperry and Tracor Flight Systems. Supersonic and manoeuvrable, this famous 'Century Series' fighter was operated over the Eglin Gulf Test Range (from Tyndall AFB) and the White Sands missile range (from Holloman AFB), until the vast majority of airframes had been destroyed during missile engagements. *(Tim Laming)*

NORTH AMERICAN F-100 SUPER SABRE

Flying for the first time on 25 May 1953, the F-100A interceptor was the USAF's first fighter aircraft capable of sustaining supersonic speeds in level flight. Powered by a Pratt & Whitney 157 turbojet (with afterburner), the aircraft was initially armed with four 20mm cannon. Some early Super Sabres were converted to RF-100A standard and were operated as photographic reconnaissance platforms, seeing limited service in Vietnam. The F-100C was a dual-role attack and interceptor variant, fitted with external stores hardpoints and an in-flight refuelling probe; however, the main production variant of the Super Sabre was the F-100D, which was nuclear-capable and equipped with AIM-9B Sidewinder air-to-air missiles. More than 1,000 F-100Ds were constructed in just two years, and the 'Delta' model saw extensive service with the USAF, not least with the Air National Guard, from which the type was finally retired during the late 1970s. The Super Sabre was also exported to Taiwan, Turkey, Denmark and France.

Following the type's retirement from ANG service, a decision was made in 1979 to convert a substantial number of F-100s to unmanned target drone standard, and some 100 aircraft (including a small number of F-100F twin-seaters) were modified by Sperry Flight Systems in Arizona. Another 240 aircraft were converted to QF-100 standard by Tracor Flight Systems at Mojave in California, over the 1986–1990 period. The QF-100s were operated from Tyndall AFB in Florida, flying target missions in support of fighter pilot training and missile test work, over the Eglin Gulf Test Range. A small number of aircraft were also assigned to Holloman AFB in New Mexico, in support of the White Sands Missile Range. The majority of the QF-100 fleet has now been destroyed during missile engagements, and converted F-106 interceptors are now assigned to the target drone role. The QF-100 is still active in civilian hands, operated by Tracor Flight Systems on a variety of test assignments and in support of NATO interceptor training activities at Decimomannu, Sardinia. The F-100 has long since been retired from active service with the air forces of France, Denmark and Turkey, although a handful of F-100D and F-100F Super Sabres may still be operational in Taiwan.

Although the USAF has ended its association with the QF-100, Tracor Flight Systems continues to maintain a small number of aircraft, most notably in Europe, in support of NATO operations (aircraft are currently deployed to Decimomannu in Sardinia). After exhausting supplies of F-100s in the States, Flight Systems turned their attention to Turkey as a potential source of airframes for conversion to drone standard. An initial batch of aircraft (including *N2011M* as illustrated) was flown to the USA via the UK, but the ferry flights suffered more than a fair share of technical problems, and later deliveries were shipped directly to the States. *(Boudewijn Pieters)*

CONVAIR QF-106 DELTA DART

Following the design and construction of the F-102 Delta Dagger, Convair embarked upon the development of a totally new interceptor, taking advantage of the latest area-rule technology and powerplant improvements. The USAF ordered the aircraft as the F-102B but a completely different interceptor emerged, the F-106A Delta Dart, featuring the same wing, but with a new fuselage (area-ruled to reduce transonic drag), revised intakes and a broader square-topped tail-fin. The radar, fire control and missile system was also new, together with the much more powerful Pratt & Whitney J75-P-17 24,500 lb thrust turbojet.

The first aircraft (no prototypes as such were constructed) flew for the first time on 26 December 1956, entering service with the USAF's Air Defense Command in July 1959. Some 277 airframes were constructed together with sixty-three twin-seat (tandem layout, unlike the TF-102's side-by-side arrangement) F-106B combat trainer derivatives. The F-106 was an unqualified success with the service life extending over thirty years, during which time further improvements to the aircraft were made, including new weapons systems, new ejection seats, an internally mounted 20mm cannon and a sensitive infra-red seeker. The aircraft continued to fly with Air National Guard units into the late 1980s, despite deliveries of F-15 Eagles.

As the aircraft were gradually withdrawn through the 1980s, the USAF selected the F-106 as a new target drone, destined to replace the QF-100, supplies of which were slowly being exhausted. An initial batch of ten aircraft was converted to drone configuration in 1990 by Honeywell, and further aircraft were converted in situ at Davis-Monthan AFB, from where the aircraft were withdrawn from storage at the AMARC (Aerospace Maintenance and Regeneration Center). Further work on the aircraft was completed in St Louis, prior to delivery to Tyndall AFB or Holloman AFB.

A total of 194 aircraft was included in the drone conversion programme, and the aircraft are now in service with the 82nd Tactical Aerial Targets Squadron at Tyndall AFB in Florida, supporting test and training missions in the Eglin Test Range. A smaller number of QF-106s also supports activities at the White Sands Missile Range, based at nearby Holloman AFB in New Mexico. The QF-106 FSAT (Full Scale Aerial Target) offers greater speed and manoeuvrability over the older QF-100 (all of which have now been destroyed or withdrawn). A small number of twin-seat QF-106Bs have also been included in the drone programme, used primarily for (manned) pilot continuation training, and both the single and twin-seat Delta Darts look set to remain in service (albeit in slowly diminishing numbers) for some considerable time, as no successor drone programme has yet been initiated.

ABOVE:
The Convair F-102 served the United States Air Force with distinction, and following its retirement from service with Air Defense Command, the Delta Dagger survived in small numbers at Tyndall AFB in Florida, where a fleet of PQM-102A unmanned target drones were gradually consumed by the missiles of visiting fighter aircraft. The F-102's grey colour scheme (or SE Asia camouflage, or even an overall greeny-brown on some examples) livened up with liberal applications of gloss red paint, makes the drone easily identifiable. *(Scott Van Aken)*

OVERLEAF:
The Convair F-106 Delta Dart also ended its USAF service life as a target drone, and some examples are still flying from Tyndall AFB, with the 475th WEG. The QF-106 acts as a highly manoeuvrable and supersonic target aircraft, and often survives numerous missile engagements. Almost 200 conversions to unmanned drone standard were made, and the aircraft continues to fly from Tyndall AFB and Holloman AFB (supporting activities at the White Sands missile range), although numbers have gradually diminished, and Phantoms are now slowly assuming the unmanned target role. *72504*'s rudder reveals its previous owners, the Massachusetts ANG. *(Scott Van Aken)*

NORTH AMERICAN F-86 SABRE

The F-86 Sabre has earned a place in American aviation history as the first USAF transonic fighter, flying for the first time on 1 October 1947. The Sabre entered USAF service in 1949 as the F-86A, powered by a 4,850 lb thrust General Electric J47-GE-1 turbojet which, together with a sleek, swept-wing design, gave the aircraft a performance which was comparable to the MiG-15 fighter encountered in the skies over Korea. More than 5,000 Sabres were constructed, and a small number of aircraft are believed to be still operating in second-line roles with the air forces of Bolivia and Honduras. Experience in Korea led to the development of the F-86E and F-86F, the latter variant becoming the most successful and combat-effective version of the Sabre, and most surviving examples are 'Foxtrot' models.

Fitted with a more powerful 5,910 lb thrust J47-GE-27 engine, the F-86F wing leading edges were fitted with slats to improve performance and the F-86H introduced four 20mm cannon, instead of the earlier six 12.7mm fit.

Although the Sabre enjoyed a long and hugely successful career with the USAF, the aircraft did not serve operationally with the US Navy, although a 'navalised' development (Fury) was flown by both the US Navy and Marine Corps. Small numbers of F-86F Sabres were operated by the USN, however, in the form of unmanned target drones, used for missile firing trials. Fitted with telemetry and remote control equipment, these QF-86F Sabres were mostly former JASDF (Japan Air Self-Defence Force) aircraft converted to the unmanned target configuration.

Based at the Naval Air Warfare Center Weapons Division at China Lake and Point Mugu in California, the Sabres were used to provide high-speed manoeuvrable targets for weapons trials programmes. As these trials continued, more and more Sabres were eventually destroyed and stocks of suitable airframes for drone conversion were eventually exhausted. The Navy is now embarking upon a similar drone conversion programme on former USN and USMC F-4N Phantoms.

LEFT:
Surprisingly, the North American F-86 Sabre was still very much in business some four decades after its entry into USAF service. The US Navy NAWC/WD (Naval Air Warfare Center/Weapons Division) operated a relatively large fleet of former ANG, Japanese, Korean, Canadian and South African Sabres, which were gradually converted to QF-86 drone configuration. They were operated from China Lake and Point Mugu as unmanned target drones in support of various air-to-air missile trials. However, the stock of Sabres slowly dwindled, and QF-4 Phantoms are slowly taking over the Sabre's role. *(Scott Van Aken)*

BELOW:
This QF-86H evidently survived at least nine attempts at destruction by missile, and survived to earn an honourable retirement from service at China Lake. She can now be seen at Chino, as part of the ever-growing collection of preserved aircraft based there. Hopefully the aircraft will eventually be restored to her former glory and, who knows, she might even fly again one day; anything's possible at Chino! *(Tim Laming)*

The Westland Sea King might not be regarded as being part of the world of aerial combat, but the Airborne Early Warning-dedicated Sea King AEW2 does play an important part in many air defence exercises. This airborne radar platform enables controllers to vector fighters on to targets, giving the Navy a useful over-the-horizon picture of radar traffic, and of course, the Sea King is able to deploy on their fleet of through-deck cruisers. *(Westland)*

WESTLAND SEA KING

Following production of the successful Wessex design, Westland continued its licence-building arrangement with Sikorsky to cover production of their SH-3 Sea King as an anti-submarine warfare platform for the Royal Navy. Four SH-3s were delivered to Westlands in 1967 and were used as engineering and systems development aircraft, leading to the production of the first Sea King HAS-1 with Rolls-Royce Gnome turboshaft engines. This aircraft flew for the first time on 7 May 1969 with deliveries to the Fleet Air Arm at Culdrose beginning in August of the same year.

Westlands' development of the Sea King has led to a wide range of specialised variants, the most recent of which bear little connection with the basic SH-3 design produced by Sikorsky. The Sea King Mk 2 with uprated engines (and six-blade tail rotor) was followed by the Mk 3 for the Royal Air Force (for search-and-rescue missions) and the Mk 4 commando assault derivative for the Royal Navy (with fixed undercarriage). Further developments to onboard systems continue through the Mk 5 and beyond, together with a variety of export versions to countries such as Egypt, Qatar, Australia, Belgium, West Germany, India, Norway and Pakistan.

The 1982 Falklands conflict highlighted a serious deficiency in airborne early warning capability which the Royal Navy had been forced to accept since the retirement of its Gannet AEW force deployed upon the now defunct HMS *Ark Royal* conventional carrier. Reliance was placed on the RAF's fleet of aged Shackleton radar platforms which were dependent upon a suitably placed land base (the Shackletons could not be refuelled in flight), and when HMS *Sheffield* was destroyed by an Exocet missile launched from a low-flying Argentine Super Etendard, it was clear that the Navy required a shipborne AEW platform. The solution was to develop an AEW version of the Sea King, and the Thorn EMI Searchwater radar was chosen as the appropriate system.

In an eleven-week programme known as Project LAST (Low Altitude Surveillance Task), two Sea King HAS-2s were suitably modified to house the radar in an inflatable Kevlar-impregnated fabric radome attached to the fuselage side. The radome is hinged to rotate downwards for operation in flight, and two radar operators are housed in the Sea King cabin. These two aircraft were embarked upon HMS *Illustrious* in August 1982 and the design was found to be highly effective, leading to an order for a further six aircraft which are now in regular Fleet Air Arm service.

BOEING E-3 SENTRY

Another development of the famous Boeing 'Dash Eighty' demonstrator, the E-3 Sentry was a derivative of the civil 707 airframe, the first such aircraft being designated EC-137D flying for the first time in February 1972. Two such aircraft were operated by the USAF to evaluate two competing radar systems for the AWACS (Airborne Warning and Control System) programme, the winning system being developed by Westinghouse. In January 1973 the USAF authorised development of the AWACS airframe and the first E-3A Sentry took to the air for the first time on 31 October 1975, the first aircraft entering USAF service during March 1977 at Tinker AFB, Oklahoma.

The E-3A was assigned to the defence of continental USA in January 1979 when NORAD personnel began augmenting Tactical Air Command personnel on missions flown from Tinker AFB. The aircraft has been deployed to bases around the world including Keflavik in Iceland, Kadena AB in Japan and Elmendorf AB in Alaska. Aircraft have also been deployed to Saudi Arabia on a regular basis, and five aircraft were eventually purchased by the Royal Saudi Air Force.

Some thirty-four Sentries were delivered to the USAF and the final (1,010th) Boeing 707 airframe has been retained by the manufacturer for further E-3 developmental work. Following the cancellation of the Airborne Early Warning Nimrod programme (initiated to replace the RAF's obsolete Shackleton fleet), the British Ministry of Defence announced an order for six E-3D Sentries on 18 December 1986, exercising an option for a seventh aircraft in October 1987. The first RAF E-3D made its maiden flight on 11 September 1989 and arrived in the UK during November 1990. Official handover to the RAF took place at Waddington on 24 March 1991, where No. 8 Squadron re-formed on the type after retiring the last Shackleton aircraft at Lossiemouth.

The E-3D, referred to as the Sentry AEW Mk 1 in RAF service, carries a flight crew of four and a specialist crew of thirteen, although this latter figure can vary according to the type of mission being flown. The rotating pod attached to the upper fuselage contains a Westinghouse AN/APY-2 surveillance radar and IFF/TADIL-C antennae. Additionally, Loral 1017 ESM pods are attached to the wingtips. USAF E-3s were used operationally during the Gulf War and RAF E-3s fly regular missions over the former Yugoslavia, normally operating directly to and from Waddington. E-3s also equip the multinational NATO AWACS force and France has become the final customer for the Sentry, the last of a long line of Boeing 707 airframes being delivered to the Armée de l'Air.

BRITISH AEROSPACE SHACKLETON

The illustrious Shackleton was the last in a line of 'heavies' designed and manufactured by A.V. Roe which could be traced back through the Lincoln and Lancaster to the Manchester twin-engined bomber. Developed in response to a Royal Air Force requirement for a long-range maritime patrol and anti-submarine warfare aircraft, the Shackleton MR1 entered service in February 1951. Essentially a World War Two-era design, the aircraft featured an unpressurised fuselage, a traditional tailwheel undercarriage layout, and machine-gun armament. Unusually however, the four Rolls-Royce Griffon engines drove twin three-blade contra-rotating propellers, giving the aircraft a characteristic 'growl' which will remain in the memories of anyone who ever heard (or flew in) the Shackleton.

The aircraft was developed into the Shackleton MR2 and, ultimately, into the Shackleton MR3 which featured a revised tricycle undercarriage layout, wingtip-mounted fuel tanks and other equipment improvements. Shackleton MR3s were exported to South Africa, and later RAF Shackletons were fitted with Viper turbojets in the outer engine nacelles, giving the aircraft a sprightly take-off performance. Unfortunately, however, these jet engines also rapidly depleted the aircraft's wing fatigue, and the Shackleton MR3s were withdrawn over the 1969–1970 period as Hawker Siddeley Nimrods were brought into service.

A small number of Shackleton MR2s remained active however, and twelve aircraft were converted to the Airborne Early Warning role during the 1971–4 period. Fitted with ancient APS-20F(I) radar first flown in 1944 (and subsequently fitted to Fleet Air Arm Skyraiders and Gannets), the Shackleton AEW2 was intended to be an interim AEW aircraft to plug a gap in the RAF's air defence capability until a purpose-built AEW aircraft could be developed or purchased. Unfortunately, political indecision and developmental setbacks (mostly centred on the radar system) led to endless delays in the production of the Airborne Early Warning Nimrod, and the latter type was eventually abandoned.

The RAF was finally equipped with Boeing E-3D Sentries, at which stage the remaining fleet of six Shackletons was retired. One aircraft was retained in flying condition by a civilian owner based in Cyprus, and the South African Air Force restored an MR3 to flying condition in 1983. Unfortunately, however, this aircraft crashed en route to an airshow appearance in the UK during 1944 and was effectively destroyed, although a second aircraft is expected to be restored as a replacement. Two former RAF AEW2s are being ferried to the United States for certification, after which they will hopefully return to the UK as civilian-owned 'warbirds'.

ABOVE:
The venerable Avro Shackleton has long since retired from RAF service, after serving for many years with No. 8 Squadron at Lossiemouth in the Airborne Early Warning role. Acting as an airborne command and control post, the Shackleton enabled fighter controllers to vector RAF and other NATO interceptors on to individual targets, and the ancient Shackleton was a part of every air defence exercise, operating alongside high-tech fighters such as the F-16, F-15 and Tornado. The AEW task has now been handed over to the Boeing E-3D Sentry and the Shackleton has gone, although one machine still makes occasional ventures into the air under the careful ownership of a civilian based in Cyprus. *(Tim Laming)*

RIGHT:
The Fleet Air Arm's Sea Harrier squadrons also operate from Yeovilton, when not embarked upon the Navy's through-deck cruisers. Tasked with multi-role fighter, ground attack and reconnaissance operations, the relatively unsophisticated Harrier is an outstanding fighter, thanks to its surprising reserve of power, small size, agility, and the famous 'VIFF' (Vectoring In Forward Flight) capability (swivelling the engine nozzles downwards whilst turning, giving the aircraft an awe-inspiring turn performance). The Sea Harrier squadrons regularly fly one-versus-one air combat sorties, as illustrated by this duo, heading out over Cornwall, complete with bolt-on refuelling probes. *(Tim Laming)*

BRITISH AEROSPACE SEA HARRIER

Following the gradual demise of the Royal Navy's aircraft carrier fleet, the British Government became set against the concept of any new combat aircraft types for the Fleet Air Arm, believing that future airpower projection could be effectively undertaken by the Royal Air Force. The Fleet Air Arm effectively became an all-helicopter force until the idea of 'through-deck cruisers' was developed around the Harrier design.

Whilst the Royal Navy's 'Invincible' class of warships are in effect 'mini aircraft carriers', the Fleet Air Arm's fighting capability was restored through the development of the Sea Harrier, a navalised version of the RAF's Harrier GR3. With a revised nose section (placing the pilot higher, to give better all-round visibility) housing a 'Blue Fox' multi-mode radar, the Sea Harrier was equipped with a new navigation and attack system, tailored for maritime operations. The airframe and engine were 'marinised' and deck hold-down anchors were added. Some thirty-four aircraft were ordered followed by a further twenty-three airframes (approximately ten aircraft are believed to have been lost/withdrawn).

Development of the naval Harrier didn't begin until 1975, thanks largely to Government indecision, and it was fortunate that the Sea Harrier finally entered service shortly before the United Kingdom went to war with Argentina in 1982; they were deployed to the South Atlantic in defence of the British Task Force. The Sea Harriers were employed extensively on air defence missions and ground attack sorties over the Falkland Islands, and it is doubtful whether the operation to retake the Islands could have been successfully completed without the Sea Harrier force.

Now deployed onboard HMS *Invincible*, *Illustrious* and *Ark Royal*, the Sea Harriers are undergoing a mid-life upgrade to FA2 standard, with a much-improved 'Blue Vixen' pulse Doppler radar, a comprehensive electronic warfare suite, and a weapons fit which will include 25mm Aden cannon, AIM-9L Sidewinders, ASRAAM short-range missiles, AIM-120A AMRAAM radar-guided medium-range missiles, together with conventional free-fall and retarded bombs.

Overseas sales of the Sea Harrier have been small, the only export customer being India, some twenty aircraft being delivered to the Indian Navy including four Harrier T60 twin-seat trainers (not fitted with radar). Further development of navalised Harriers has been concentrated on the McDonnell Douglas/British Aerospace AV-8B airframe.

MCDONNELL DOUGLAS A-4 SKYHAWK

Designed in response to the United States Navy requirement for a carrier-based attack aircraft, the A-4 was one of a series of classic aircraft designs created by Ed Heinemann, and one which immediately secured US Navy interest leading to an order for two XA4D-1 prototypes and eighteen YA4D-1 test airframes. The first prototype made its maiden flight on 22 June 1954 and deliveries of the initial A4D-1 production version (later redesignated A-4A) began in 1956.

The US Navy expected their new attack aircraft to be turboprop-powered, and it was Heinemann's radical approach to aircraft design which led to the lightweight turbojet-powered Skyhawk (the prototype was powered by a Wright 65, a licence-built Armstrong Siddeley Sapphire), which exceeded the required payload and performance figures at just half the anticipated weight. The A4D-1 (165 built) was followed by 542 A4D-2 (A-4B) aircraft, capable of carrying Bullpup air-to-surface missiles and featuring a navigation and bombing computer. Some sixty-six aircraft were later refurbished and transferred to Argentina as A-4P and A-4Q Skyhawks, many of which saw service during the 1982 Falklands conflict. Further A-4Bs were rebuilt as A-4S Skyhawks for Singapore with 30mm cannons replacing the standard US Navy 20mm weapons.

The A-4C introduced further improvements such as an autopilot and terrain-avoidance radar and some 638 airframes were constructed, the majority of which saw service with the USN and USMC during the Vietnam War. Some aircraft were later converted to A-4L standard, with an avionics refit and J65 engines. The A-4E (with a J52 engine) was followed by the A-4F which introduced a 'zero-zero' ejection seat, lift dumpers and spoilers and additional cockpit armour. The similar A-4G was exported to Australia and the A-4K was sold to New Zealand (A-4Es were sold to Israel).

OPPOSITE:
VFC-13, the *Saints*, are based at Miramar NAS, a Naval Air Reserve unit tasked with adversary training duties. The *Scooter* is rapidly nearing the end of its service life with the US Navy, and a mix of F-14s and F/A-18s are destined ultimately to replace the Skyhawk in the aggressor role. *(Tim Laming)*

BELOW:
A VF-126 bird wearing Cuba's national flag on her tail. Under the fuselage is an Air Instrumentation pod which records the air combat manoeuvring mission for post-flight debriefing, enabling the crews to replay the whole mission on a video screen, as viewed from any position required. *(Tim Laming)*

The Skyhawk was produced in tandem-seat dual-control versions, the first NTA-4F flying in June 1965, retaining the same performance capabilities as the single-seat Skyhawk versions. Twin-seat derivatives of export versions were also manufactured, the most unusual being Singapore's TA-4S which featured a separate second cockpit and canopy. TA-4J trainers remain active with the US Navy, pending further deliveries of T-45 Goshawks. The 'ultimate' A-4 design was the A-4M (with an uprated J52 engine), leading to further export versions as well as the improved A-4Y for the USMC. The A-4M and A-4Y (together with TA-4J and TA-4F twin-seaters) remain in use with the US Navy and US Marine Corps as aggressors, albeit in small numbers.

ABOVE:
A-4F *154209* from VF-126 wears yet another bizarre camouflage scheme, pictured as she zooms over the freeway running along Miramar's airfield perimeter. VF-126 passed the aggressor role to VFC-13 and the latter unit is likely to move to Lemoore NAS when Miramar's Tomcat squadrons move out, Topgun moves to Fallon, and the base is handed over to the United States Marine Corps.
(Tim Laming)

RIGHT:
Unusual view of an A-4F tucked behind a KC-10 over the California desert. This view emphasises the late model Skyhawk's characteristic 'hump', which houses an electronic package, including an Angle Rate Bombing System which was a valuable part of the *Scooter*'s capability during her days in the bombing role.
(Curtiss Knowles)

ABOVE:
VFC-13, the *Fighting Omars*, are based at Oceana, tasked with dissimilar air combat training duties. Their small fleet of dark-grey-painted A-4M and A-4F Skyhawks was expanded during 1994 when VF-43 disestablished and handed over their aggressor role (and no doubt some of their aircraft) to the *Omars*. The Skyhawk's days at Oceana will soon be over however, and VFC-13 will probably receive F/A-18s.
(Joel Paskauskas)

RIGHT:
Deep in the heart of Texas, Dallas Naval Air Station is the home of two Reserve F-14 Tomcat squadrons and a Marine F/A-18 unit. Until recently, the Base Flight operated a small fleet of A-4M Skyhawks in support of these units, flying dissimilar air combat missions in the local area. Sadly, the Tomcats, Hornets and Scooters will be leaving Texas soon, as the base appears to have fallen victim to a recent round of defence expenditure cutbacks.
(Scott Van Aken)

DOUGLAS A-3 SKYWARRIOR

Designed in response to a 1947 US Navy requirement for a carrier-capable strategic strike and attack bomber, the Douglas XA3D-1 Skywarrior prototype flew for the first time on 28 October 1952. Powered by a pair of Westinghouse XJ40-WE-3 turbojets, the powerplant was switched to the Pratt & Whitney J57 following the failure of the former engine. The first production variant of the Skywarrior was the A3D-1 (later redesignated A-3A), making its maiden flight in September 1953, entering service with the US Navy during March 1956. Only a relatively small number of aircraft were manufactured, and the US Navy effectively standardised on the later A-3B, which remained active with US Navy strike units well into the 1960s.

Further modifications to the A-3B airframe resulted in the KA-3B, an in-flight refuelling tanker assigned to Carrier Air Wings, and the EKA-3B, a similar tanker variant with additional electronic countermeasures capability. These specialised Skywarrior variants remained active with the Navy even after all bomber-assigned A-3s had been withdrawn by the late 1960s. The RA-3B was a photographic reconnaissance variant,

VAQ-33 operated a fleet of three Douglas ERA-3B Skywarriors as communication jammers and threat simulators. The enlarged tail section housed a chaff dispenser, and under the fuselage, a large pod contained an AN/ALT-40 Airborne Electronic Warfare System, consisting of a jammer, direction finder, receiver and control unit. Also visible is one of the four ram air turbines, which provided power for the electronic equipment. *(Gary Meinert)*

Complete with Soviet-style insignia, a VAQ-34 ERA-3B Skywarrior (*144841*) bakes in the California sunshine at NAF El Centro during March 1990. With a threat emitter pod attached to the wing pylon, this low-vis camouflaged machine has now been retired, and the venerable 'Whale' has been completely removed from US Navy service, although a small number of Skywarriors remain active with civilian operators. *(Scott Van Aken)*

which although largely successful was quickly replaced by the RA-5C Vigilante. Surplus reconnaissance Skywarriors were converted into ERA-3B ECM platforms, or assigned to test/developmental work (NRA-3B). A small number of former TA-3B navigator/bombardier trainers were later converted into high-speed VIP transports, remaining active with the US Navy into the 1980s.

The Skywarrior ended its US Navy career as a specialised ECM platform, operated by VQ-2 (Rota), VAQ-33 (Key West) and VAQ-34 at Point Mugu. Carrier operations ended in 1987 following the loss of two EA-3Bs, one being destroyed during a night landing on the USS *Nimitz*. Political pressure encouraged the Navy to restrict the Skywarrior to land-based operations (even though the aircraft was still carrier-capable) and the last carrier landing by a Skywarrior was made aboard the USS *Ranger* on 21 November 1987. The Skywarrior continued to fly in the ECM role until 1992, when Lockheed ES-3A Vikings began delivery to the USN, enabling the EA-3B fleet to be retired. Various test aircraft continued to operate with the US Navy; however, by the mid-1990s these aircraft have mostly been withdrawn into storage pending possible future use if necessary. One aircraft continues to fly with the US Army on test duties at Holloman AFB, whilst a small fleet of Skywarriors is assigned to Hughes on missile development work, based at Van Nuys airport. Other Skywarriors continue to fly periodically on various experimental duties, with civilian operators.

LOCKHEED T-33

Without doubt, the Lockheed T-33 was the most successful jet trainer aircraft ever built, more than 6,000 having been constructed and operated by more than twenty countries, and after forty years the 'Tee Bird' is still flying. Developed from the Lockheed F-80 Shooting Star (the first jet-powered aircraft to become operational with the US Army Air Force), the aircraft was essentially a stretched-fuselage derivative, featuring a tandem twin-seat cockpit arrangement, originally designated TF-80C.

After becoming operational with the United States Air Force, numbers of T-33s soon outstripped the F-80 from which the aircraft was derived, and the T-33 became the USAF's standard jet trainer throughout the 1950s. Almost 700 aircraft were also delivered to the United States Navy under the designation TO-2, eventually redesignated TV-2 and then T-33B (late in 1962). Many aircraft were supplied to overseas air arms, mainly through the Military Assistance Programme, and the T-33 saw service with France, Greece, Portugal, Italy, Spain, Turkey and West Germany (amongst others) through the MAP system. Licence production of the T-33 was undertaken in Canada and more than 600 CL-30 Silver Stars were produced, many of which remain in service with the Canadian Armed Forces as the CT-133, mostly used for electronic aggressor, communications and liaison flying. Likewise, Japan produced the aircraft under licence, and from a total of 210 aircraft a small number are still active.

The ubiquitous Lockheed T-33 is still active around the world, albeit in relatively small numbers. The Canadian Armed Forces operates a fleet of CT-133 Silver Stars, many of these aircraft being utilised as electronic warfare trainers. *133560* is one of No. 414 Squadron's EW platforms (an ET-133) pictured during September 1990, resplendent in the most recent Canadian low-visibility camouflage colours. *(Peter Foster)*

Also part of No. 414 Squadron's T-33 fleet, *133174* received an eye-catching paint scheme during 1991, with the squadron's emblem on the nose and a huge maple leaf motif on the aircraft's undersides. What a pity that other NATO forces don't allow individual squadrons to show such great spirit! *(Tim Laming)*

Like many other military aircraft designs, the T-33 was developed for missions other than basic flying training. The RT-33A was a specialised single-seat photographic reconnaissance aircraft which was operated by France, the Netherlands and Turkey amongst others. A close air support and interdiction variant was also produced, designated AT-33A, some examples of which are still active with smaller air arms around the world. The Tee Bird also saw extensive service as a target drone, ending years of service life as an unmanned, radio-controlled target over the Pacific Missile Test Center range, or over the Naval Weapons Center range. Often controlled by an airborne operator in a DT-33 director aircraft, these aircraft supported a variety of weapons trials programmes until they were inevitably destroyed by an air-to-air missile. The Skyfox Corporation proposed the re-manufacturing of the T-33 airframe for re-sale or extended service life, based around externally mounted Garrett TFE731 turbofan engines and a strengthened and modified airframe. Although the Skyfox design was largely successful, the aircraft was not ordered into production, no doubt due to a wealth of competing 'new-build' trainer designs being readily available.

GRUMMAN F-14 TOMCAT

An aggressor's-eye-view of a typical 'customer' in the shape of a Grumman F-14A Tomcat from VF-51, the 'Screaming Eagles', based at Miramar in California. VF-51 pilots and aircraft were responsible for most of the flying sequences in the motion picture *Top Gun*, flying representative air combat manoeuvring profiles with various A-4 and F-5 aggressors. *(Grumman)*

Following the cancellation of the troubled F-111B programme, the US Navy issued a requirement for a new carrier-capable fighter, and from a short list of four submissions Grumman's G-303 design was selected, resulting in the first flight of the F-14A on 21 December 1970. Twelve development aircraft were constructed, enabling Grumman to continue work on the Tomcat flight test programme after the prototype was destroyed on its second flight, following a catastrophic hydraulic failure. Production F-14As reached completion stage in 1972, the first aircraft going to VF-125 at Miramar during October of that year. Operational deployments began in September 1974 when the first aircraft were deployed on board the USS *Enterprise* with VF-1 and VF-2.

Some 557 F-14As were constructed for the US Navy, together with eighty aircraft for Iran, although it is doubtful whether few, if any, of these aircraft remain airworthy after many years of political isolation from the West. At peak strength the F-14A equipped thirty USN fighter squadrons distributed between the Atlantic and Pacific fleets with shore bases at Oceana and Miramar. The F-14B, originally designated F-14A+, retained the avionics fit of the F-14A but with F110 turbofan engines. Some thirty-eight aircraft were manufactured by Grumman, with an additional thirty-two aircraft being converted from 'Alpha' model airframes. The latest version of the Tomcat is the F-14D, the first examples reaching squadron service in November 1990. Plans were made to convert more than 400 F-14As to F-14D standard but current plans are for just eighteen aircraft to be converted, combined with thirty-seven new-build examples.

OPPOSITE:
F-14 Tomcats are fairly recent additions to the NFWS fleet, and F-14A *159607* has become the most eye-catching bird on the Miramar ramp, resplendent in Imperial Iranian Air Force colours. Adversary units regularly paint aircraft in representative colour schemes as part of an ongoing effort to provide 'realism' for the aggressor role, and this Tomcat's colours are particularly appropriate, as the Iranian AF continues to operate a small fleet (spares permitting) of F-14As. *(Ted Carlson)*

BELOW:
Another show-stopper from the NFWS fleet, F-14A Tomcat *159855* appeared during 1992 disguised as a Russian Su-27. The effect was fairly convincing, and during one stopover at an air base in the States, the resident security forces were sure that they were looking at a real 'Flanker'. Sadly, the aircraft was involved in a ground accident, and the fake-Sukhoi colour scheme hasn't reappeared . . . so far. *(Scott Van Aken)*

An outstanding interceptor, the Tomcat is armed with a variety of weapons, the primary system being the Hughes AIM-54 Phoenix, a long-range AAM capable of destroying virtually any type of target at any height/aspect. For medium-range engagements the Tomcat carries AIM-7M Sparrows which will be gradually replaced by 'fire-and-forget' AIM-120s (the Sparrow requires its target to be radar-illuminated until impact). For close-range interceptions the ubiquitous AIM-9M is employed, although a new solid-state AIM-9R version is expected to enter service soon with an improved seeker head and longer-range rocket motor.

The F-14 was employed extensively during Operation 'Desert Storm', although the Tomcat had already seen operational activity having participated in various engagements with Libyan Su-22s. Tomcats have recently been assigned to 'Top Gun' (NFWS) at Miramar, introducing the aircraft into the aggressor training role, while other Tomcats have also been modified to provide the USN with an air-to-ground capability. A small number of aircraft are also assigned to VX-4 and NAWC/WD at Point Mugu, and the NAWC/AD at Pax River.

PANAVIA TORNADO GR1/1A

The Tornado design and development programme began during 1968 when a multinational feasibility study was initiated, eventually resulting in the Multi-Role Combat Aircraft (MRCA) which flew for the first time on 14 August 1974. Following extensive developmental flying, the first production-standard aircraft were completed towards the end of the 1970s and the first Tornado GR1 for the Royal Air Force was delivered on 1 July 1980 to RAF Cottesmore, home of the TTTE (Trinational Tornado Training Establishment).

Wings fully swept, a Tornado GR1 from No. 15 Squadron, based in Germany. The unit has since disbanded, re-forming at Lossiemouth as No. 15(R) Squadron, the Tornado Weapons Conversion Unit. Tornado GR1s play an important part in many exercises, flying attack missions against airfields, radar and SAM sites, and other strategically important targets. In addition to a pair of underwing fuel tanks, this aircraft is carrying a BOZ chaff/flare dispenser and a Sky Shadow ECM pod.
(British Aerospace)

The Tornado GR1 is numerically and tactically the Royal Air Force's most important aircraft, a low-level strike and attack weapons platform designed to replace the Vulcan in the strike role, and both the Canberra and much of the Jaguar fleet in the tactical offensive support role. The aircraft are assigned to NATO and four squadrons are currently deployed to Germany, based at RAF Bruggen, with a reserve unit based in the UK (assigned to weapons conversion training). Tornado GR1s are equipped with a variety of weaponry, ranging from 1,000 lb free-fall or laser-guided bombs, BL.755 cluster bombs and JP.233 airfield denial pods to ALARM (Air-Launched Anti-Radiation Missile) and the WE177B nuclear bomb. Internal armament comprises two Mauser 27mm cannon, and self-defence capability is provided by AIM-9L Sidewinder AAMs, one of which can be carried under each wing. Other defensive equipment includes Sky Shadow ECM pods and the BOZ-107 chaff/flare dispenser.

The Tornado GR1A is a day/night all-weather tactical reconnaissance aircraft, developed from the 'Alpha' model. Flying for the first time during July 1985, the GR1A entered RAF service in May 1987 and now equips Nos. 2 and 13 Squadrons based at RAF Marham. The GR1A carries no optical camera equipment and relies exclusively on synthetic electro-optical sensors which provide better all-weather performance and facilitate easier interpretation. Recorded video film can be replayed in flight, or transmitted to a ground unit in 'real time' if necessary, and the aircraft retains its combat capability although the twin Mauser cannon fit has been removed in order to accommodate the reconnaissance sensors. The Tornado GR1A was used operationally for the first time during the Gulf War in 1991.

The Tornado GR1B has replaced the Buccaneer in the maritime strike role, some twenty-four aircraft having been modified to carry four (eventually five) Sea Eagle anti-ship missiles, retaining the GR1A's combat capability and acquiring the Buccaneer's 'buddy-buddy' in-flight refuelling capacity. The Tornado GR4 is the latest (and probably the ultimate) derivative of the basic IDS (Interdictor/Strike) airframe, and applies to RAF Tornado GR1s which will undergo a mid-life update towards the end of the decade.

PANAVIA TORNADO F3

Developed as part of the multinational MRCA programme, the Tornado ADV (Air Defence Variant) was designed in response to the Royal Air Force's requirement for a long-range stand-off interceptor. Although both the Lightning and Phantom were well-established in RAF service during the 1970s, both aircraft were approaching obsolescence and neither possessed a true long-range interception capability. The Tornado ADV was designed specifically to undertake combat air patrols at huge distances from the mainland United Kingdom, and to be able to maintain such patrols for extended periods. Armed with the British Aerospace Sky Flash AAM, the aircraft would be capable of intercepting incoming hostile bombers at BVR (Beyond Visual Range) distances.

So much for the theory; unfortunately the concept of a BVR interceptor was flawed and did not take into account the very real possibilities of close-in 'dogfighting' scenarios. The Tornado ADV programme proceeded however, but by the time the aircraft entered Royal Air Force service it was becoming clear that the RAF had acquired the right aircraft for the wrong job. Worse still, the Tornado ADV's development programme was plagued with problems and delays which earned the aircraft an unenviable (and largely unfair) reputation as a proverbial 'white elephant'. The first Tornado F2s were delivered to RAF Coningsby in 1984, equipped with Turbo Union RB199-34R Mk 103 engines each delivering 16,920 lb thrust and a weapons fit of four Sky Flash and four AIM-9L Sidewinders, together with an internal 27mm cannon.

With a top speed in excess of Mach 2, the Tornado F2 might not have been a highly manoeuvrable dogfighter, but it was certainly a sprightly interceptor. Sadly, the performance of the AI-24 Foxhunter radar did not match the airframe's impressive performance, and continual delays in radar development led to many Tornado F2s being delivered to the RAF without any radar, a block of concrete ballast occupying the fighter's nose cone (leading to sarcastic press references to the F2's 'Blue Circle' radar). The fleet of eighteen F2s was quickly replaced by large-scale deliveries of Tornado F3s, with uprated Mk 104 engines, automatic wing sweep, and a fully functioning Foxhunter radar, although problems with the latter equipment continued for some time and it wasn't until the early 1990s that the RAF finally acquired what was effectively a fully capable Tornado F3 force. Now established in RAF service F3 will remain in use until the Eurofighter (in whatever form) finally becomes operational with the RAF, at which stage the Tornado F3 is certain to be swiftly withdrawn. The Tornado F3 is an outstanding interceptor (especially in the hands of an experienced RAF pilot), but the RAF is unlikely to mourn its eventual demise.

A 23 Squadron Tornado F3 in action, firing her Mauser cannon at the hessian banner target being towed by a 100 Squadron Canberra PR7. This particular Canberra was a former 13 Squadron reconnaissance machine, modified for banner target towing. The Canberra TT18 was able to carry the more sophisticated Rushton winched target which could be deployed and recovered in flight, and now that the TT18 has gone (and No. 100 Squadron has moved from Wyton to Leeming), the unit (and therefore the RAF) no longer possesses this capability. *(Paul Jackson)*

LEFT:
An unusual view of two Tornado F3s from No. 23 Squadron, pictured during a transit flight to RAF Akrotiri, after completing an air combat sortie over the Mediterranean. With wings partially swept, the Tornado's sleek lines emphasise the fact that the F3 possesses an all-out low-level top speed which cannot be matched by virtually any other fighter type. *(Paul Jackson)*

BELOW:
Over the North Sea, a pair of Tornado F3s from No. 11 Squadron take on fuel from a VC10 tanker. The Tornado F3 force has recently been reduced to a total of six squadrons, together with an Operational Conversion Unit (following the disbandment of No. 23 Squadron), and it's likely that another F3 squadron will soon be withdrawn, reducing the RAF's fighting force still further. *(Tim Laming)*

RIGHT:
Navigator's-eye-view of a Tornado F3, and yes, the Tornado F3's refuelling probe is installed on the *port* side of the nose. This picture was taken from a 111 Squadron Phantom FG1 during a Tornado-versus-Phantom air combat exercise, high over the North Sea. The Phantom's refuelling probe is safely plugged into a VC10 tanker's hose basket, while the fuel flows. *(Tim Laming)*

BELOW:
An interesting (and nostalgic) picture from September 1987, showing a pair of No. 229 OCU Tornado F2s in company with a pair of Binbrook-based Lightnings, taking fuel from a 55 Squadron Victor tanker during an air defence exercise. The Lightnings and Victors are all now retired, and the Tornado F2 has been withdrawn into long-term storage, while No. 229 OCU has become No. 56(R) Squadron. Binbrook has also closed. *(Tim Laming)*

Pictured over the Mediterranean, a trio of Tornado F3s from No. 11 Squadron head for RAF Akrotiri, to begin a two-week stay at an APC (Armament Practice Camp). While based in Cyprus, the squadron flew air combat manoeuvring sorties, and flew live cannon firing sorties in company with a banner-towing aircraft from No. 100 Squadron. Each RAF Tornado squadron deploys to Akrotiri for an APC on a rotational basis. The beautifully decorated *ZE764* was repainted in more conventional camouflage colours for operations in the Gulf, and sadly, the colour scheme was never re-applied. *(Paul Jackson)*

Breaking away from the camera ship, a Tornado F3, with wings fully swept, reveals the under-fuselage housings for up to four Skyflash missiles, and underwing rails for up to four AIM-9 Sidewinders. Controversy still surrounds the Tornado F3, concerning its relatively modest performance when compared to agile fighters such as the F-16 and F-15. Unfortunately, the Tornado F3 is the 'right aircraft for the wrong role', in that it was designed to fly long-range intercepts against a threat which has now largely disappeared. There's no doubt that as a BVR (Beyond Visual Range) interceptor, the F3 is a great aeroplane, but the RAF is eagerly anticipating the arrival of a new-generation fighter in the shape of the Eurofighter. *(Paul Jackson)*

LOCKHEED L-1011 TRISTAR

The Lockheed L-1011 began life in 1966 as a design study concept, originally twin-engined but later changed to the familiar three-engine layout. The first flight took place on 16 November 1970 but just weeks later the powerplant manufacturer (Rolls-Royce) went into receivership, throwing the TriStar programme into confusion. Lockheed was also suffering from severe financial difficulties at the time, and it was only through governmental and customer airline assistance that both companies survived. The TriStar emerged as a successful airline design, but didn't enjoy a particularly impressive sales record thanks to a worldwide recession and heavy increases in fuel costs, combined with fierce competition from Boeing's 747 and McDonnell Douglas's DC-10. A total of 250 airframes was constructed and the last aircraft rolled out on 19 August 1983.

No. 216 Squadron's Tristars provide the RAF with an effective strategic transport capability, flying missions all around the world. One of the more regular Tristar routes is from Brize Norton to Mount Pleasant on the Falkland Islands, and during these flights No. 1435 Flight often mount practice interception missions, using the incoming Tristar as a suitable target. Pictured in January 1992, a Phantom escorts a Tristar to Mount Pleasant, after intercepting the transport en route from the UK. The Phantoms have now been replaced by Tornado F3s.
(Andy Evans)

Royal Air Force interest in the TriStar was prompted by a pressing need for increased refuelling tanker capability, highlighted by the 1982 Falklands conflict when the RAF Victor force was severely overstretched in terms of operational commitments, leading to rapid conversions of Hercules and Vulcan aircraft to tanker configuration, prior to the introduction of the VC10 tanker fleet. Six L-1011-500 aircraft were purchased from British Airways and were converted by Marshalls to TriStar K1 tanker/passenger (four aircraft) and TriStar C2 tanker/passenger/freighter (two aircraft) standard.

The conversion to tanker configuration involved the installation of underfloor fuel tanks, boosting internal fuel capacity to 300,000 lb. An unusual twin HDU (Hose Drum Unit) was fitted in the lower rear fuselage and a refuelling probe (together with the associated fuel system) was attached to the fuselage above the flight deck. The first K1 conversion flew on 9 July 1985 and was transferred to Boscombe Down for service trials during the following month. The first aircraft to enter RAF service joined a re-formed 216 Squadron at Brize Norton on 24 March 1986.

Two K1 aircraft are currently in regular service, configured for passenger transport and tanker support. Four KC1s (including two additional aircraft purchased from the now defunct Pan American Airways) are configured for combined passenger and cargo-carrying operations with a 140 x 102 inch cargo door fitted into the fuselage wall, and a roller conveyor system capable of accepting up to twenty pallets, or seating for up to 196 passengers. The aircraft also have a refuelling tanker capability. Two C2 transports are also in service, carrying up to 265 passengers and 35,000 lb of freight, and these aircraft are expected to be fitted with underwing refuelling pods in due course.

BRITISH AEROSPACE VC10

Although developed primarily as a transatlantic airliner, the Vickers VC10 has also become a major element of the Royal Air Force's transport and refuelling tanker force, and a total of fourteen aircraft was constructed specifically for the RAF. Flying for the first time in June 1962, the VC10 was purchased by BOAC, BUA and East African Airways, the first RAF aircraft flying in November 1965. Although featuring a shortened fuselage, the VC10 C1 is essentially a Super VC10 as flown in airline service.

As the fleet of VC10 C1s approach the end of their service lives, they have been retrofitted with underwing refuelling pods, enabling the aircraft to perform tanker duties as well as their more regular strategic transport commitments. It is likely that the aircraft will soon be withdrawn entirely from the transport role, concentrating instead on the tanker mission (with the designation VC10 C1K). Although the VC10s were equipped from the outset to receive fuel in flight, it is only in recent years that the aircraft have been permanently fitted with bolt-on refuelling probes, giving the strategic transports an even greater range and flexibility.

During 1978 the Ministry of Defence opted to purchase redundant VC10 airliners for conversion into air-to-air refuelling tankers, and a second batch of VC10s is currently under conversion to this role. The VC10 K2 designation applies to five former Gulf Air type 1101s which were refurbished by British Aerospace at Filton, the first conversion flying in June 1982. Fitted with two underwing Mk 32 Hose Drum Units and a centreline-mounted Mk 17B HDU, the aircraft is also equipped with a closed circuit TV system, enabling the crew to monitor refuelling operations from the flight deck.

The VC10 K3 designation applies to four type 1154 Super VC10s formerly operated by East African Airways, and converted by British Airways during 1982–1984. The K3 features a longer fuselage and retains the cargo door fitted to the type 1154. Inboard thrust reversers have been removed in order to standardise the VC10 fleet. The internal layout varies considerably from the VC10 K2 layout, most notably in the cockpit where a navigator's position has been added (the position was 'standard' in the K2). VC10 K4s are former British Airways Super VC10s which were stored at RAF Abingdon for many years, prior to commencing tanker conversion. The future of the VC10 fleet is assured, although it is quite likely that the K2 fleet may be withdrawn at a relatively early stage, followed by the C1K fleet.

RIGHT:
The classic lines of the Vickers VC10, against a sunny seascape. The Royal Air Force is the sole user of this elegant airliner design, with a fleet of VC10 K2, K3 and K4 aircraft dedicated to aerial refuelling tanker support. No. 10 Squadron's fleet of VC10 transports are also being progressively converted to twin-point tanker configuration, and will probably abandon most, if not all, of their strategic transport duties. *(Tim Laming)*

BRITISH AEROSPACE VICTOR

One of the Royal Air Force's famous trio of 'V-Bombers', the Handley Page Victor first flew on Christmas Eve 1952, the third of the classic strategic bomber designs. Some fifty Victors were constructed in an initial B Mk 1 variant, followed by thirty-four Victor B Mk 2s with more powerful engines, larger wing span, new internal systems and a capability to carry the Blue Steel stand-off nuclear bomb. In company with the Vulcan, the Victor Mk 2 fleet formed part of Britain's nuclear deterrent until the late 1960s.

The fleet of Vickers Valiant bombers, after having been assigned to air-to-air tanker operations, was withdrawn in 1964 following the discovery of extensive airframe fatigue in most of the Valiant fleet. This resulted in an urgent requirement for new tanker aircraft and Victor B1s were quickly converted to this role, equipped with two underwing hose drum unit pods. Following the withdrawal of the Victor B2 and SR2 from the bomber and strategic reconnaissance role, more tanker conversions were initiated. Handley Page became bankrupt in 1970 which resulted in a fleet of twenty-four Victors being ferried to Avro's airfield at Woodford (where the Vulcan, ironically, had been built) for conversion into three-point tankers (two underwing Mk 20A pods and a centreline-mounted Mk 20B pod under the rear fuselage).

Weapons systems were removed together with the electronic countermeasures fit and other equipment. Structural improvements were made, including reduction of the wing span, and the fuel system was completely replaced, with fuel tanks occupying the former bomb-bay. Equipped with a total of nineteen fuel tanks (including two huge externally mounted underwing tanks), the Victor K2 carried a total of 100,000 lb of transferable fuel. During the 1982 Falklands conflict the Victor fleet was heavily involved, supporting virtually every flight to and from the South Atlantic, as the 'new' VC10 tanker fleet had yet to enter regular service. Having been rapidly fitted with Omega and Carousel navigational aids, the Victors also undertook long-range reconnaissance missions, and one aircraft performed a record-breaking radar reconnaissance mission from Ascension Island to Grytviken and South Georgia, the longest sortie in aviation history (over 7,000 miles).

Victors were also heavily involved in the support of other Falklands combat missions including the famous Vulcan 'Black Buck' bomber and anti-radar sorties, but the conflict took a heavy toll in terms of fatigue life, and the Victor fleet gradually dwindled until late 1993 when the type was finally withdrawn from Royal Air Force service at RAF Marham.

OPPOSITE:
Another classic aircraft, the beautiful crescent-winged Victor, making a farewell appearance for the camera late in 1993, shortly before retirement. Although designed as a strategic nuclear bomber, the Victor became better known as a refuelling tanker, supporting countless training missions and exercises, and refuelling dozens of different fighter, transport, maritime and ground attack types. *(Tim Laming)*

BELOW:
The Victor played an important part in the air defence of the United Kingdom for many years, flying refuelling missions with RAF fighters scrambled from Leuchars, Leeming, Binbrook, Coningsby and Wattisham, during intercept 'scrambles' against Soviet aircraft approaching UK airspace. The long-range nature of these sorties meant that every mission required a refuelling tanker to support the fighters, and until the introduction of the VC10, the Victor was the RAF's only tanker aircraft type. Sadly, all have now been retired, and most have been scrapped, with just four aircraft surviving intact. *(Tim Laming)*

DE HAVILLAND SEA VIXEN

Developed in response to both Royal Navy and Royal Air Force requirements, de Havilland's DH 110 was essentially a 'scaled up' development of the successful Vampire design, retaining the same twin-boom tail configuration but with swept-back wings and twin-engine powerplants. Ministry of Supply interest in the design led to an order for seven land-based night-fighter prototypes and two long-range fighter derivatives, all for the RAF, while a further two examples of each type were ordered for the Fleet Air Arm. By way of a 'back-up', four examples of the Gloster GA 5 were also ordered for the RAF. The RAF order was later reduced to two examples of each DH 110 variant together with two GA 5s, but RAF interest began to concentrate on the GA 5 which later entered RAF service as the Javelin fighter. The DH 110, however, continued to interest the Royal Navy.

Two prototype DH 110s were constructed at Hatfield, the first making its maiden flight on 26 September 1951, exceeding Mach 1 during a test flight on 9 April 1952. It appeared at the 1952 Farnborough SBAC show but was destroyed in a catastrophic accident on 6 September.

The wing structure failed during a high-speed turn, and the aircraft crashed into crowds of spectators, killing twenty-nine, together with pilot John Derry and observer Tony Richards. The second prototype was immediately grounded and was eventually strengthened accordingly before re-entering the test programme in 1953. During February of the following year an order was placed for a semi-navalised DH 110 prototype which first flew on 20 June 1955.

A production order for seventy-eight aircraft was placed in January 1955, including a batch of twenty-one developmental aircraft, all redesigned to specification N.139P for a high-performance all-weather fighter. The airframe was approximately eighty per cent redesigned and the powerplant selection was made in favour of a pair of Avon 208s, each developing 10,000 lb thrust. The DH 110 was the first British fighter not to be armed with guns, Firestreak AAMs being the aircraft's primary armament. On 5 March 1957 the aircraft was named 'Sea Vixen' and the first production aircraft was rolled out in February 1957 at Christchurch, making its first flight (to nearby Hurn) on 20 March. After a series of intensive service trials with No. 700Y Flight, the latter unit was re-commissioned as No. 892 Squadron on 2 July 1959, embarking on HMS *Ark Royal* the following year. Further development of the design led to the Sea Vixen Mk 2, with additional fuel capacity and Red Top AAM armament, and the first production aircraft made its first flight on 8 March 1963, service deliveries beginning in 1963. The Sea Vixen's FAA operational career ended in 1972, although a small number of aircraft remained active on a variety of developmental projects. The only remaining airworthy Sea Vixen was a manned/unmanned D 16 target drone operated by the DRA, although it was withdrawn during 1995.

MCDONNELL F-101 VOODOO

Originally developed for service with Strategic Air Command fighter units, the Voodoo eventually served with most USAF combat commands including TAC, ADC, PACAF and USAF as well as the Air National Guard, the Canadian Armed Forces and the Chinese Nationalist Air Force. An important and versatile fighter design, it was also a particularly important aircraft for the manufacturer, the Voodoo being their first aircraft to be accepted for production by the USAF.

OPPOSITE:
The de Havilland Sea Vixen was for many years the mainstay of the Fleet Air Arm's defensive capability, and the type has long since disappeared into history ... well, not quite – just one example remains semi-active with the Defence Research Establishment at Llanbedr in Wales. Used as a target drone airborne control aircraft (and, if necessary, as an unmanned target drone itself), *XP924* was maintained in flying condition, although actual flying operations appear to have ended. *(John Hale)*

ABOVE:
Perhaps *the* most famous electronic warfare aircraft, *101067* was the last airworthy McDonnell Voodoo, pictured in 1984 shortly before she was retired (disappointing aircraft nuts all around the world). Although this EF-101B was a USAF machine, it was operated by the Canadian Armed Forces as part of No. 414 Squadron, an an EW platform, until the unit re-equipped with Canadair Challengers. *(Peter Foster)*

Developed from an existing experimental design (the XF-88 Voodoo), the Advanced Voodoo featured more powerful Pratt & Whitney J57 turbojets, increased fuel capacity and in-flight refuelling equipment for both receptacle and probe receiving. The new design was incorporated into a mock-up which was completed in 1952. An initial production contract for twenty-nine F-101As was signed on 28 May 1953 and the first aircraft made its maiden flight from Edwards AFB on 29 September 1954, going supersonic during the flight. The F-101A was later developed into the RF-101A reconnaissance platform before attention switched to the twin-seat F-101B, an all-weather interceptor powered by afterburning (16,900 lb thrust) J57 engines. The revised nose design housed an MG-13 fire control system and gave the aircraft an all-missile armament, including two MB-1 Genie AAMs with nuclear warheads. Making its first flight in March 1957, the F-101B was developed into the F-101F with infra-red detection equipment and an upgraded fire control system.

The CF-101B designation applied to fifty-six F-101Bs delivered to the RCAF in 1961–62. During 1971 the forty-six surviving airframes were exchanged for fifty-six former USAF Voodoos, one of which became the world's last flying example, an EF-101F assigned to No 414 Squadron. The former Canadian aircraft were modified into twin-seat reconnaissance aircraft, redesignated RF-101B, and served with the Nevada ANG prior to replacement by RF-4Cs. The F-101C was designed specifically for the nuclear strike role, strengthened for low-level operations with Tactical Air Command. Retaining the same engine and armament as the F-101A, the 'Charlie' models regularly had the internal 20mm cannon removed and replaced by Tacan equipment.

Voodoos served extensively with the USAF during the Vietnam War, and RF-101s flew regular missions during the 1962 Cuba missile crisis. The F-101B continued to serve with Air National Guard units until the late 1970s and CF-101B remained active with the Canadian Armed Forces until the early 1980s. Just one aircraft was assigned to civilian test research duties, with the Colorado State University.

BRITISH AEROSPACE VULCAN

Without doubt the mighty Vulcan was an impressive machine, the last in a long line of 'heavies' designed by the A.V. Roe Company (Avro) in Manchester. Following the initial development of an atomic bomb, the British Government required a high-speed and long-range bomber which would be capable of delivering such a weapon to targets in the Soviet Union. Unusually, no less than three competing designs were selected for production, this famous trio of 'V-Bomber' types comprising the Valiant, Vulcan and Victor.

Avro design work drew on German experience with delta-winged projects, and in an effort to reduce the risks of such an advanced design programme, a series of scaled-down research aircraft was produced. The first full-scale prototype Avro 698 (later named 'Vulcan') made its maiden flight from Avro's airfield at Woodford on 30 August 1952. The first production Vulcan B1 was rolled out at Woodford in January 1955, flying for the first time on 4 February, some twelve months ahead of Handley Page's Victor. Entry into RAF service took place on 30 July 1956 when the first aircraft joined No. 230 Operational Conversion Unit at RAF Waddington. Development of the Vulcan continued, resulting in the more powerful and manoeuvrable B2 which entered service on 1 July 1960. The B2 was capable of carrying twenty-one 1,000 lb free-fall bombs, or a single free-fall nuclear weapon. Much of the B2 fleet was later modified to carry the Avro Blue Steel stand-off nuclear missile, while other B2s were assigned to carriage of the Douglas Skybolt missile which was later cancelled before reaching operational status.

Although the United Kingdom's nuclear deterrent passed into the hands of the Royal Navy at the end of the 1960s, the Vulcan force remained operational in the nuclear strike role until the 1980s when the Vulcan squadrons finally began to disband. At this late stage the Vulcan was hurriedly returned to operational service during the 1982 Falklands conflict, flying ultra-long-range bombing missions over the Falklands from Ascension Island. Radar attack missions were also flown, and Vulcans were quickly converted into single-point refuelling tankers, remaining active in this role until 1984 when the Vulcan finally retired from operational service. One aircraft was retained for appearances at airshows however, such was the Vulcan's outstanding public popularity, and it wasn't until 1993 that this aircraft was finally retired and sold to a civilian buyer.

RIGHT:
XH558 was the first Vulcan B2 to enter Royal Air Force service, and was the last to leave the RAF in 1993, having survived retirement as a one-off airshow performer, thrilling crowds all around the UK. After serving as both a conventional and nuclear bomber, the aircraft was modified to B2(MRR) standard, serving with No. 27 Squadron as a Maritime Radar Reconnaissance platform. (Tim Laming)

LEFT:
After serving with No. 27 Squadron as a reconnaissance aircraft, *XH558* was modified by British Aerospace for operations as a single-point refuelling tanker, in 1982. Emerging from the former Avro factory as a Vulcan K Mk 2, the aircraft retained its reconnaissance capability and was occasionally seen carrying underwing air sampling pods, whilst still performing the tanker role. Following the disbandment of No. 50 Squadron, *XH558* was retained by the RAF as an airshow performer, finally retiring in 1993. She is now the subject of a long-term refurbishment programme, and will hopefully fly again in civilian hands, from her new home at Bruntingthope in Leicestershire. *(Mike Jenvey)*

The mighty Vulcan also played its part as an 'aggressor', acting as a hostile intruding bomber in many RAF and NATO exercises. *XM575* of No. 44 Squadron is pictured climbing away from home base at RAF Waddington in Lincolnshire during an exercise in 1982. The huge delta-winged bomber sometimes encountered NATO interceptors and was more than a match for many fighter pilots, who couldn't match the Vulcan's altitude, turning performance, or staggering rate of descent. *(Mike Jenvey)*